Mental illness and criminal
behavior

DATE DUE

At Issue

Mental Illness and Criminal Behavior

Other Books in the At Issue Series:

At Issue

Mental Illness and Criminal Behavior

Shannon Fiack, Book Editor

GREENHAVEN PRESS
A part of Gale, Cengage Learning

NEW ENGLAND INSTITUTE OF TECHNOLOGY
LIBRARY

GALE
CENGAGE Learning™

Detroit • New York • San Francisco • New Haven, Conn • Waterville, Maine • London

\#310171801

Christine Nasso, *Publisher*
Elizabeth Des Chenes, *Managing Editor*

For more information, contact:
Greenhaven Press
27500 Drake Rd.
Farmington Hills, MI 48331-3535
Or you can visit our Internet site at gale.cengage.com

Articles in Greenhaven Press anthologies are often edited for length to meet page requirements. In addition, original titles of these works are changed to clearly present the main thesis and to explicitly indicate the author's opinion. Every effort is made to ensure that Greenhaven Press accurately reflects the original intent of the authors. Every effort has been made to trace the owners of copyrighted material.

Cover image by Illustration Works.

LIBRARY OF CONGRESS CATALOGING-IN-PUBLICATION DATA

Mental illness and criminal behavior / Shannon Fiack, book editor.
    p. cm. -- (At issue)
  Includes bibliographical references and index.
  ISBN 978-0-7377-4434-7 (hbk.)
  ISBN 978-0-7377-4435-4 (pbk.)
  1. Mentally ill offenders. 2. Violent crimes--Psychological aspects. 3. Violence--Psychological aspects. I. Fiack, Shannon.
  HV6133.M455 2009
  364.2'4--dc22
                                                                2009006082

Printed in the United States of America
1 2 3 4 5 6 7 13 12 11 10 09

Contents

Introduction

In 1843, a Scottish man named Daniel M'Naughten killed Sir Robert Peel, secretary to the British prime minister. M'Naughten was attempting to murder the prime minister himself. More significant than the attempted assassination was the subsequent legal trial: M'Naughten employed the insanity defense, and the case shaped the rules of the defense for years to come. Initially, the jury found M'Naughten not guilty by reason of insanity. A panel of judges reviewed the ruling at the Queen's behest and, in finding M'Naughten guilty, established rules about insanity pleas that remained in effect for more than one hundred years. The "M'Naughten test" required that for insanity to be a defense, the defendant must either not understand the nature of his act or not understand that the act is wrong.

As the field of psychiatry grew, the rules for insanity pleas were gradually expanded, until the 1980s when they again changed in response to a failed assassination attempt. John Hinckley Jr., shot at President Ronald Reagan, wounding him and three other men. Hinckley stated that his crime was an attempt to impress actress Jodie Foster. He was found not guilty by reason of insanity, prompting lawmakers to toughen the rules for insanity pleas. Courts shifted back to a stricter rule similar to the M'Naughten test, which made employing the defense more difficult.

The debate continues over how the law should treat those suffering from mental illness. Those opposed to the defense claim that it is often abused. Carol Valentine, in her article "The Insanity of the Insanity Defense," argues "the insanity defense is used consciously to escape the penalties of the law." It is a "defense of last resort," she quotes a U.S. attorney, "the only time it's used is when there is no question the accused committed the act, and the defense can think of nothing else."

Opponents also contend that expert testimony from doctors is a sham: the defense can always find a psychiatrist willing to say the defendant is mentally ill, and the prosecution's doctor will say the opposite. In his book *The Myth of Mental Illness*, Thomas Szasz goes further, arguing that mental illness is not an illness at all, but merely a failure to cope with normal life. Thus, it is no reason to hold people less responsible for their crimes.

Supporters of the insanity defense claim the plea is necessary, and not overused. Although high-profile cases—Ted Kacyznski (the Unabomber), John A. Muhammed (the Beltway Sniper), and Lorena Bobbit—receive a great deal of publicity, less than one percent of all criminal defendants plead not guilty by reason of insanity. In only a quarter of those instances does the plea successfully lead to acquittal.

Many mental health organizations support the belief that it is morally wrong to punish people who do not understand the nature or gravity of their conduct. Laws hold children to different standards of behavior and prohibit the execution of the mentally retarded. The insanity plea is consistent with this approach—that it is not ethical to punish those who cannot comprehend the consequences of breaking the law.

Another aspect of this debate is how to treat criminals with mental illness. Prison conditions can exacerbate symptoms, and needed medical care is rarely available. An alternative is confinement in psychiatric care facilities. Advances in both the understanding and treatment of mental illness have resulted in higher quality modern hospitals. Gone are the days when such places were as bad as prisons, and "patients" were held in windowless rooms and often restrained more than they were treated. (M'Naughten was condemned to spend his final twenty-one years in such a place.) However, some argue that mentally ill convicts get off too easily when sentenced to care facilities; they deserve punishment and should suffer in prison just like other criminals. A compromise was developed in the aftermath of the Hinckley trial: a dozen states created the guilty but mentally ill (GBMI) verdict. A defendant who is found GBMI is sent to a mental institution until he is satisfactorily treated, after which he is transferred to prison to serve his time.

Sadly, many detention facilities are not properly equipped to handle people with mental illnesses. A lack of proper treatment can lead individuals to reoffend as their conditions worsen. Kelsey Patterson was executed in Texas in 2004 for a double murder in 1992. Patterson was clearly delusional and suffering from paranoid schizophrenia. He had committed numerous violent assaults throughout the 1980s, but his illness was never addressed. As the *Houston Chronicle* put it, he was "left half-treated and unsupervised by the state for years despite a history of psychotically inspired, near-fatal assaults." Many argue that society can prevent crimes like Patterson's by treating mental illness within the criminal justice system.

Valid defense or not, mental illness is a causal factor in many crimes. But is there a relationship on a grander scale? Are people suffering from mental illness more likely to commit crimes? Surprisingly, there is a scarcity of research on the subject. However, studies that have been conducted tend to show correlations between certain types of mental illness and certain types of crime. The prevalence of mental illness in prison populations is higher than that in the general population. Mentally ill offenders are most likely to have committed acts of assaultive violence or sexual offenses.

Since before M'Naughten's time, society has addressed the issue of how to deal with those whose criminal behavior is driven by mental illness. Aspects of the debate include how to hold them accountable, how to treat their illnesses, and how to deal with correlations between illness and criminal behavior. The authors of the viewpoints in *At Issue: Mental Illness and Criminal Behavior* investigate the various facets of the modern debate on this topic.

1

Mental Illness and Substance Abuse Increase the Risk of Violence

Richard A. Friedman

Richard A. Friedman, M.D., is a professor of clinical psychiatry and the director of the psychopharmacology clinic at Weill Cornell Medical College, New York.

Statistics show that people with certain mental illnesses are prone to exhibiting violent behavior. However, substance abuse is more likely than mental illness to cause violence, and the combination of the two is even more highly correlated with violence. Proper treatment, including medication, can reduce the risk of violence among the mentally ill. Mandatory treatment, although controversial, is one option for reducing the risk.

On Sunday afternoon, September 3, 2006, Wayne Fenton, a prominent schizophrenia expert and an associate director at the National Institute of Mental Health (NIMH), was found dead in his office. He had just seen a 19-year-old patient with schizophrenia who later admitted to the police that he had beaten Fenton with his fists.

This tragic incident was widely publicized and raises, once again, the controversial question about the potential danger posed by people with mental illness. The killing also left many in the mental health and medical communities concerned

Richard A. Friedman, "Violence and Mental Illness—How Strong Is the Link?" *New England Journal of Medicine*, vol. 355, no. 20, November 16, 2006, pp. 2064–2066. Copyright © 2006 Massachusetts Medical Society. All rights reserved. Reproduced by permission.

about their own safety in dealing with psychotic patients. After all, if an expert like Fenton, who understood the risks better than most, could not protect himself, who could?

It is not an idle question. According to the National Crime Victimization Survey for 1993 to 1999, conducted by the Department of Justice, the annual rate of nonfatal, job-related, violent crime was 12.6 per 1000 workers in all occupations. Among physicians, the rate was 16.2 per 1000, and among nurses, 21.9 per 1000. But for psychiatrists and mental health professionals, the rate was 68.2 per 1000, and for mental health custodial workers, 69.0 per 1000.

For Tim Exworthy, a forensic psychiatrist at Redford Lodge Hospital in London who was recently assaulted by a patient, the risk of job-related violence is no longer a dry statistic. He was beaten unconscious by a 19-year-old psychotic man whom he had been treating in the hospital for 5 months. "I was talking with him in a room and telling him why he couldn't leave, when I was suddenly aware of a few blows to my head," recounted Exworthy. "The next thing I knew, I was at the nursing station wiping the blood off my face. I never saw this coming and hadn't anticipated that he would react like that."

Patients with serious mental illness—those with schizophrenia, major depression, or bipolar disorder—were two to three times as likely as people without such an illness to be assaultive.

Such attacks by psychotic patients highlight a larger question: Are people with mental illness really more likely than others to engage in violent behavior? If so, which psychiatric illnesses are associated with violence, and what is the magnitude of the increase in risk?

Posing these questions is itself not without risk: being perceived as dangerous can have a devastating effect on a person's prospects for relationships, employment, housing, and social functioning. People with mental illness already bear the burden of much social stigma, and I am loath to add to it. But without a realistic understanding of this risk, medical practitioners can neither provide the best care for their patients nor ensure their own safety when the clinical situation warrants it.

Until recently, most studies have focused on the rates of violence among inpatients with mental illness or, conversely, the rates of mental illness among people who have been arrested, convicted, or incarcerated for violent crimes.[1] For example, one national survey showed that the lifetime risk of schizophrenia was 5% among people convicted of homicide—a prevalence that is much higher than any published rate of schizophrenia in the general population—suggesting an association between schizophrenia and homicide conviction.[2] These studies, however, tend to be limited by selection bias: subjects who are arrested, incarcerated, or hospitalized are by definition more likely to be violent or very ill and thus are not representative of psychiatric patients in the general population.

Substance abuse among the mentally ill compounds the increased risk of violence.

A more accurate and less biased assessment of the risk of violence perpetrated by the mentally ill comes from epidemiologic studies of community samples. The best known is the NIMH's Epidemiologic Catchment Area (ECA) study, which examined the rates of various psychiatric disorders in a representative sample of 17,803 subjects in five U.S. communities. Although this study was not initially designed to assess the prevalence of violent behavior, data on violence were collected for about 7000 of the subjects.[3] "Violence" was defined as having used a weapon such as a knife or gun in a fight and having become involved, with a person other than a partner or spouse, in more than one fight that came to blows—behavior that is likely to frighten most people.

The study showed that patients with serious mental illness—those with schizophrenia, major depression, or bipolar disorder—were two to three times as likely as people without such an illness to be assaultive. In absolute terms, the lifetime prevalence of violence among people with serious mental illness was 16%, as compared with 7% among people without mental illness. Although not all types of psychiatric illness are associated with violence—anxiety disorders, for example, do not seem to increase the risk—and although most people with schizophrenia, major depression, or bipolar disorder do not commit assaultive acts, the presence of such a disorder is significantly associated with an increased risk of violence.

Of course, because serious mental illness is quite rare, it actually contributes very little to the overall rate of violence in the general population; the attributable risk has been estimated to be 3 to 5%—much lower than that associated with substance abuse, for example. (People with no mental disorder who abuse alcohol or drugs are nearly seven times as likely as those without substance abuse to report violent behavior.) But substance abuse among the mentally ill compounds the increased risk of violence: one study involving 802 adults with a psychotic or major mood disorder showed that violence was independently correlated with several risk factors, including substance abuse, a history of having been a victim of violence, homelessness, and poor medical health.[4] The 1-year rate of violent behavior for subjects with none or only one of these risk factors was 2%—a prevalence close to the ECA study's estimate for the general population. Thus, violence in people with serious mental illness probably results from multiple risk factors in several domains.

Much can be done to diminish the risk of violence among the mentally ill. A study that compared the prevalence of violence in a group of psychiatric patients during the year after hospital discharge with the rate in the community in which the patients lived showed no difference in the risk of violence between treated patients and people without a psychiatric disorder.[5] Thus, symptoms of psychiatric illness, rather than the diagnosis itself, appear to confer the risk of violent behavior. So patients with schizophrenia who are free of the acute psychotic symptoms that increase this risk, such as having paranoid thoughts or hearing voices that command them to hurt others (called command auditory hallucinations), may be no more likely to be violent than people without a mental disorder. The study did not specifically monitor the treatments, but it seems possible that treating psychiatric illness does not just make patients feel better; it may also drastically reduce the risk of violent behavior.

In the wake of Fenton's killing, there may be renewed efforts to expand the criteria or lower the clinical threshold for mandatory treatment of patients with psychosis—a movement that is sure to be controversial. We know that most such patients are not violent, but we also know that a patient with acute psychosis who is paranoid and has command auditory hallucinations or a history of being violent, being a victim of violence, or abusing alcohol or drugs is at high risk for violent behavior. Currently, in order to protect civil liberties, most states mandate treatment (whether hospitalization or medication) only if there is unambiguous evidence of an immediate danger to others, which is generally interpreted as overt threats or violent actions. Perhaps it makes sense to reset the threshold at the presence of known clinical risk factors—psychotic thoughts that are influencing behavior, a history of violence, and significant concurrent substance abuse. But expanding the criteria would require further substantiation that these factors can be accurately identified by clinicians and that their use in mandating treatment is warranted. The possibility that expanding the criteria might also discourage people with psychotic illnesses and substance abuse problems from voluntarily seeking treatment would also need to be considered.

It is natural for psychiatrists and other medical professionals who treat psychiatric patients to deny, to some extent, the possible danger. After all, it is hard to have a therapeutic relationship with a patient we fear. Still, we need to remind ourselves that the risk of violence, though small, is real, and we must take necessary precautions. As Exworthy put it, "I guess I let down my guard and paid for it." Keeping up our guard means paying attention to our fear and anxiety about a patient; no physician should ever treat a patient whom he or she fears. It also means seeing patients with acute psychosis in locations where there is adequate assistance and security, such as hospitals and clinics, rather than in a private office setting.

The challenge for medical practitioners is to remain aware that some of their psychiatric patients do in fact pose a small risk of violence, while not losing sight of the larger perspective—that most people who are violent are not mentally ill, and most people who are mentally ill are not violent.

References

1. Monahan J. Mental disorder and violent behavior: perceptions and evidence. Am Psychol 1992;47:511–21.

2. Shaw J, Hunt IM, Flynn S, et al. Rates of mental disorder in people convicted of homicide: national clinical survey. Br J Psychiatry 2006;188:143–7.

3. Swanson JW. Mental disorder, substance abuse, and community violence: an epidemiological approach. In: Monahan J, Steadman HJ, eds. Violence and mental disorder: developments in risk assessment. Chicago: University of Chicago Press, 1994:101–35.

4. Swanson JW, Swartz MS, Essock SM, et al. The social-environmental context of violent behavior in persons treated for severe mental illness. Am J Public Health 2002;92:1523–31.

5. Steadman HJ, Mulvey EP, Monahan J, et al. Violence by people discharged from acute psychiatric inpatient facilities and by others in the same neighborhoods. Arch Gen Psychiatry 1998;55:393–401.

2

Mental Illness and Crime Cannot Be Compared Due to Varying Definitions

Herschel Prins

Herschel Prins is a visiting professor of criminology at Loughborough University and honorary professor at the University of Birmingham, both in the United Kingdom.

Relationships exist between various mental illnesses and violent crime. Affective disorders, hypomanic disorder, and mental impairment may lead to instances of violent criminal behavior. Mental health professionals have a duty to explore these relationships and encourage better public understanding of the intersection of mental illness and criminal behavior.

From time to time, persons charged with a grave offence such as homicide are found to be suffering from severe depressive disorder at the time of the offence. [O.J.] West, in his study of cases of *Murder Followed by Suicide*, suggested that sufferers from such (psychotic) depression may:

> become so convinced of the helplessness of their misery that death becomes a happy escape. Sometimes, before committing suicide, they first kill their children and other members of the family. . . . Under the delusion of a future without hope and the inevitability of catastrophe overtaking their nearest and dearest as well as themselves, they decide to kill in order to spare their loved ones' suffering.

Herschel Prins, "Mental Disorder and Violent Crime: A Problematic Relationship," *Probation Journal*, vol. 52, no. 4, 2005, pp. 333–357. © 2005 SAGE Publications. All rights reserved. Republished with permission of Sage Publisher, conveyed through Copyright Clearance Center, Inc.

[Nikola] Schipkowensky also stressed the extent to which the 'patient feels his personality is without value (delusion of inferiority). His life is without sense, it is only [one of] everlasting suffering, and he feels he "deserves" to be punished for his imaginary crimes'.

Case Vignette 1

The *Independent* reports the case of a young mother who was found dead at the foot of a cliff in Scotland. It was said that she was suffering from severe post-natal depression. She was believed to have thrown her two children over the cliff and then killed herself. It was reported that she had a history of serious mental health problems.

Persons in full-flight hypomanic states can be some of the most potentially *dangerous people suffering from a clearly definable mental illness.*

Case Vignette 2

A young man had become severely depressed and was so convinced that the world was a terrible place in which to live that he attempted to kill his mother, his sister and then himself. Only swift medical intervention saved all their lives. Following a court appearance, he was made the subject of hospital care; he responded well to treatment and made a good recovery.

Trying to estimate the extent and duration of a depressive illness and its relevance to serious offences such as homicide is very difficult. [John] Gunn et al. put the position very clearly:

> It is very difficult to establish *unless several helpful informants are available* whether a depressed murderer is depressed because he has been imprisoned for life, depressed because of the conditions in which he has been imprisoned, depressed by the enormity of his crime, or whether he committed murder because he was depressed in the first place.

The comment by Gunn et al. emphasizes the importance of the availability of a full social history of the offender and the circumstances in which the crime was committed, a task well within the province of the probation service.

A statement by [J.] Higgins is also very important:

> Depression may result in serious violence, tension and pre-occupation building up over a protracted period and an assault committed in a state of grave psychological turmoil. The act itself might then act as a catharsis, the individual not afterwards appearing depressed nor complaining of depression *and the diagnosis then being missed.*

Cases of mild or moderate mental impairment are the most likely conditions to come to the attention of the criminal justice system.

Hypomanic Disorder and Violent Crime

Hypomanic disorder is characterized by elevation of mood, ideas (delusions) of grandiosity, lack of insight, disinhibition (often sexual) and anger if frustrated in pursuit of the sufferer's aims. From time to time, persons may come to the attention of the courts because of their outrageous, insightless and potentially dangerous behaviour. The following case vignette illustrates the nature of the condition.

Case Vignette 3

This concerned a car salesman in his twenties. He initially impressed his employer as a bright, energetic and very enthusiastic worker. However, it was not long before his ideas and activities took a grandiose and highly unrealistic turn. For example, he sent dramatic and exaggerated letters daily to a wide range of motor manufacturers. His behaviour began to deteriorate rapidly, he lost weight through not eating (he 'never had time') and he rarely slept. One night, in a fit of rage directed towards his 'unsympathetic' employer, he returned to the car showrooms, smashed the windows and did extensive damage to several very expensive cars. He appeared in court, was remanded for psychiatric reports, and was eventually hospitalized under the Mental Health Act [England and Wales].

The characteristics of this type of patient are worth re-emphasizing, since they justify the 'mental illness' label very clearly. They consider themselves to be omnipotent and become convinced that their wildest ideas are, in fact, entirely practical. Because there is no impairment of memory, they are capable of giving persuasive rationalized arguments and explanations to support their actions. It is important to stress that such persons are very difficult to treat without the use of compulsory powers, since they fiercely resist the idea that anything is wrong with them. However, though lacking insight, they can appear deceptively lucid and rational; it is this that makes their behaviour a very real risk to others. They can be not only hostile, but also physically aggressive to those they consider are obstructing them in their plans and activities. Persons in full-flight hypomanic states can be some of the most *potentially* dangerous people suffering from a clearly definable mental illness. . . .

An individual's mental impairment may be associated with a disorder that may make him or her particularly unpredictable, aggressive, and impulsive.

Mental Impairment and Violent Crime

Cases of mild or moderate mental impairment are the most likely conditions to come to the attention of the criminal justice system. In any event, as [Kenneth] Day points out, 'The contribution of the mentally handicapped to the criminal statistics is small'. He goes on to suggest that:

Although the prevalence of offending in the mentally handicapped appears to have remained unchanged over the years, increase is to be anticipated in the coming years as implementation of Care in the Community policies expose more mentally handicapped people to greater temptations and opportunities for offending and the 'hidden offences' which occur regularly in institutions become more visible.

The following is a summary of the ways in which the mentally impaired may become involved in violent crime:

- The degree of impairment may be severe enough to prevent the individual from understanding that his or her act was legally wrong. In such cases, issues of responsibility will arise and decisions will have to be made as to whether or not to prosecute the alleged offender.

- The moderately impaired individual may be more easily caught in a criminal act.

- Such offenders may be used very easily by others in delinquent escapades and find themselves acting as accomplices—sometimes unwittingly, sometimes not.

- An individual's mental impairment may be associated with a disorder that may make him or her particularly unpredictable, aggressive and impulsive.

- Some mentally impaired offenders have problems in making understood their often harmless intentions. Thus, a friendly overture by them may be misinterpreted by an uninformed or unsympathetic recipient as an attempted assault, leading to a rebuff. This may in turn lead to surprise and anger on the part of the mentally impaired individual and he or she may then retaliate with aggression.

- A moderately mentally impaired individual may be provoked quite readily into an uncharacteristic act of violence.

- The attitude to legitimate expressions of sexuality in some of the mentally impaired may be naïve, primitive, unrestrained and lacking in social skills. Such deficits may account for the number of sexual offences that appear to be found in the backgrounds of detained mentally impaired patients in the high security hospitals.

- Mentally impaired persons may be especially vulnerable to changes in their social environments that would not have the same impact upon their intellectually more able peers.

Two case vignettes illustrate some of the problems referred to above.

Case Vignette 4

A man of 26 was charged with causing grievous bodily harm to a young woman by hitting her over the head with a metal bar. She was entirely unknown to him, and though he denied the offence vehemently, he was convicted by the Crown Court [court in England and Wales] on the clearest possible evidence. As a child he had suffered brain damage, which had resulted in a mild degree of mental impairment, accompanied by the kind of impulsive, aggressive and unpredictable behaviour referred to above. He had been before the courts on a number of occasions and had eventually been sent to a hospital for the mentally handicapped. He was discharged some years later to the care of his mother. Subsequent to his discharge, he committed the offence described above and was placed on probation. His response was poor. He was impulsive and erratic, and regressed to very childish behaviour when under stress. The family background was problematic: the parents had divorced (acrimoniously) when the offender was quite small; a brother suffered from a disabling form of epilepsy; and other members of the family showed decidedly eccentric lifestyles. (Such a family today might be called 'dysfunctional'.) Shortly after the probation period expired, he committed a particularly vicious and unprovoked assault on a small girl and was sentenced to a long term of imprisonment.

Case Vignette 5

This case illustrates some of the other problems identified above. For many years, a mildly mentally impaired man in his forties had worked well under friendly but firm supervision. His work situation changed, with the result that his new employers felt he was being lazy and they did not have much sympathy for his disabilities. In addition, his new workmates teased and picked on him. One day, one of them taunted him about his lack of success with the opposite sex. Goaded beyond endurance, the defendant stabbed his tormentor in his chest with a pitchfork, causing quite serious internal injuries. When the case came to the Crown Court, evidence was given as to his mental condition, his social situation and the manner in which he had been provoked. The court made a Hospital Order under the Mental Health Act. . . .

Better Understanding Is Needed

All the conditions described in this contribution need to be viewed against the social and political climate prevailing currently. This climate is much preoccupied with public protection, the assessment of risk and the resulting over-hasty implementation of more and more criminal justice measures to deal with our current 'folk devils.' Professionals have a responsibility to keep their heads above these turbulent waters and to remain calm. Indeed, they have a responsibility, whenever they can, to promote better public understanding. However, they can only do this if they have informed knowledge. It is hoped that this article has made a modest contribution in this direction.

3

Criminals Know Right from Wrong, Regardless of Mental Illness

Stanton E. Samenow

Stanton E. Samenow is a clinical psychologist who has spent thirty years as a researcher, clinician, consultant, and expert witness specializing in criminal behavior. He has been appointed to three presidential task forces on law enforcement, victims' rights, and a drug-free America.

Criminals choose to commit their crimes. Their individual hardships, backgrounds, and circumstances, including mental illness, do not excuse their acts. The legal system needs to place blame where it belongs: on the people who commit crimes.

In nearly a half-century, little has changed in terms of deeply ingrained beliefs about the causes of crime. In the classic, still often performed, 1957 musical *West Side Story*, Stephen Sondheim parodied what then was the current thinking about juvenile delinquency in the song "Gee, Officer Krupke." Delinquents were punks because their fathers were drunks. They were misunderstood rather than no good. They were suffering from a "social disease," and society "had played [them] a terrible trick." They needed an analyst, not a judge, because it was "just [their] neurosis" acting up. In short, their criminal behavior was regarded as symptomatic of a deep-seated psychological or sociological problem. In this chapter I shall briefly discuss this proposition. In subsequent chapters I shall examine them in greater detail and show that the prevalent thinking about crime has been and still is loaded with fundamental misconceptions resulting in devastating consequences for society.

A man abducts, rapes, and murders a little girl. We, the public, may be so revolted by the gruesomeness of the crime that we conclude only a sick person could be capable of such an act. But our personal gut reaction shows no insight into, or understanding of, what really went on in this individual's mind as he planned and executed the crime. True, what the perpetrator inflicted upon this child is not "normal" behavior. But what does "sick" really mean? A detailed and lengthy examination of the mind of a criminal will reveal that, no matter how bizarre or repugnant the crime, he is rational, calculating, and deliberate in his actions—not mentally ill.

Criminals know right from wrong. In fact, some know the laws better than their lawyers do. But they believe that whatever they want to do at any given time is right for them. Their crimes require logic and self-control.

Some crimes happen so fast and with such frequency that they appear to be compulsive. A person may steal so often that others become convinced that he is the victim of an irresistible impulse and therefore a "kleptomaniac." But a thorough mental examination would show that he is simply a habitual thief, skilled at what he does. He can case out a situation with a glance, then quickly make off with whatever he wants. A habit is not a compulsion. On any occasion, the thief can refrain from stealing if he is in imminent danger of getting caught. And if he decides to give up stealing for a while and lie low, he will succeed in doing so.

The sudden and violent crime of passion has been considered a case of temporary insanity because the perpetrator acts totally out of character. But again, appearance belies reality.

A man murders his wife in the heat of an argument. He has not murdered anyone before, and statistical trends would project that he will not murder again. It is true that the date, time, and place of the homicide were not planned. But an examination of this man would show that on several occasions he had shoved her and often wished her dead. In addition, he is a person who frequently has fantasies of evening the score violently whenever he believes that anyone has crossed him. He did not act totally out of character when he murdered his wife. He was not seized by an alien, uncontrollable impulse. In his thinking, there was precedent for such a crime. An individual with even worse problems, but with a different personality makeup, would have resolved them differently. For example, one man whose family I evaluated during a child custody dispute discovered that his wife was spending hours on the Internet involved with a man whom she met and had sex with, then announced her plan to spend the rest of her life with him. Although her husband was emotionally devastated and irate, he neither threatened nor attacked her. He proceeded through the legal system toward divorce and obtaining custody of his daughter.

If criminals are not mentally ill, aren't they nevertheless victims of poverty, divorce, racism, and a society that denies them opportunities? Since the late nineteenth century, there has been a prevalent opinion that society is more to blame for crime than the criminal. But criminality is not limited to any particular societal group, as the 3.2 million arrests during 1999 demonstrate.

Sociologists assert that the inner-city youngster responds with rage to a society that has excluded him from the mainstream and put the American dream beyond his reach. Some even contend that crime is a normal and adaptive response to growing up in the soul-searing conditions of places like Watts and the South Bronx. They observe that correctional institutions contain a disproportionately large number of inmates who are poor and from minority groups. These inmates are seen as casualties of a society that has robbed them of hope and virtually forced them into crime just so they can survive.

The critical factor in becoming a criminal justice statistic is not race or ethnicity; it is the character of the individual and the choices he makes.

Suburban delinquents are also regarded as victims—of intense pressures to compete, of materialism, of parents who neglect them or push them to grow up too fast, or are overly protective. These adolescents are perceived as rebelling not only against their parents but against middle-class values, seeking meaning instead through kicks and thrills.

If it isn't grinding poverty that causes crime, then its opposite—overindulgence—is cited as the cause. As developing nations become increasingly industrialized and their citizens become prosperous, crimes that were rare burst into headlines. In a *Bangkok Post* article about two tragic shooting sprees, the writer conjectured that "Western-style teenage crime" was emerging in Thailand because Thai children were so indulged that they would "snap" when confronted by life's hardships. Whether a child is deprived or pampered tells us nothing about how he will turn out. Most children who grow up in poverty and most indulged children become independent, resourceful, and responsible.

What of the observation that a disproportionate number of people incarcerated for crimes are both poor and from minority groups? Does this make a commentary on those groups? Or does it prove that the criminal justice system is racist? To whatever extent inequities exist, they need to be corrected. During the past thirty-three years I have focused on individuals, not groups. While interviewing and evaluating members of various ethnic and racial groups, I have found that in nearly every case members of the offender's own family have been law-abiding. The critical factor in becoming a criminal justice statistic is not race or ethnicity; it is the character of the individual and the choices he makes. It is unwarranted and racist to assume that because a person is poor and black (or brown, red, or yellow) he is inadequate to cope responsibly with his environment and therefore can hardly help but become a criminal.

Peer pressure is seen as a critical factor in the lives of youngsters from all social classes who turn to crime. Experts point out that some subcultures reward being daring and tough, and not living by a work ethic. Kids learn about crime from one another; they are schooled in the streets and go along with the crowd in order to acquire self-esteem and a sense of belonging. The belief that crime is contagious like a disease is more than a century old.

Every social institution has been blamed for contributing to crime. Schools have been singled out as forcing into crime youngsters who don't fit the academic mold. Churches have been accused of not providing leadership to wayward youth and to the community at large. Newspapers, television, and the movies have been charged with glamorizing crime. American business and advertising have been accused of contributing to distorted values and therefore to crime.

Sociological explanations for crime, plausible as they may seem, are simplistic.

Economic hard times have been associated with an increase in crime. But then so have good times. Financial setbacks are said to push despondent people over the edge. But then, when times are booming, it has been thought that the gap between the "haves" and "have nots" widens and the latter, out of resentment, turn to crime. Economic pressures are also seen as contributing to crime by forcing mothers to go to work, further weakening the family. Their children have less supervision and guidance than before, and are even more vulnerable to peer pressure.

Economic adversity affects us all. We may be pushed to work longer hours or to take a second job. Women who prefer to be at home may have little choice but to go to work. Families may have to make do with less and watch goals slip further out of reach, and people on fixed incomes bear a special burden. The responsible person responds to economic pressures by sacrifice and hard work. Even for him, temptation may be stronger to step outside the law as the economic squeeze grows tighter. Ultimately, however, it comes down to how each person chooses to deal with the circumstances he faces.

Sociological explanations for crime, plausible as they may seem, are simplistic. If they were correct, we'd have far more criminals than we do. Criminals come from all kinds of families and neighborhoods. Most poor people are law-abiding, and most kids from divorced parents are not delinquents. Children may bear the scars of neglect and deprivation for life, but most do not become criminals. The environment does have some effect. For instance, it can provide greater or fewer opportunities for crime to occur—greater or lesser deterrence. But people perceive and react to similar conditions of life very differently. A family may reside in a neighborhood where gangs roam the streets and where drugs are as easy to come by as cigarettes. The father may have deserted and the mother may collect welfare. Yet not all the children in that family turn to crime. In suburbia, a family may be close emotionally and well off financially, but that is not enough to keep one of the youngsters from using drugs, stealing, and destroying property. In an area where firearms and drugs are readily available, most residents choose to use neither. The criminal seizes upon opportunities that others shun. More critical than the environment itself is how the individual chooses to respond to whatever the circumstances are.

We have seen other instances of when a major change in the environment suppresses crime or permits it to flourish even throughout an entire country. When totalitarian governments with their despots fall from power and are replaced by democratic regimes, the citizenry has more freedom. The responsible person has opportunity to develop his talents and pursue interests that he couldn't before. The person who is criminally inclined also has greater freedom and will pursue whatever interests him. This in part explains the surge in crime reported in countries that previously had oppressive governments.

Criminals claim that they were rejected by parents, neighbors, schools, and employers, but rarely does a criminal say why he was rejected. Even as a young child, he was sneaky and defiant, and the older he grew, the more he lied to his parents, stole and destroyed their property, and threatened them. He made life at home unbearable as he turned even innocuous requests into a battleground. He conned his parents to get whatever he wanted, or else he wore them down through endless argument. It was the criminal who rejected his parents rather than vice versa.

Not only did he reject his family, but he rejected the kids in the neighborhood who acted responsibly. He considered them uninteresting, their lives boring. He gravitated to more-adventurous youngsters, many of whom were older than he. Crime is not contagious like chicken pox. Even in crime-infested neighborhoods, there are youngsters who want no part of the action. Sure, there is the desire to belong to the crowd, but the question is which crowd. Criminals are not forced into crime by other people. They choose the companions they like and admire.

The school does not reject the antisocial youngster until he is impossible to deal with. Many criminals have no use for school whatsoever. Some remain in school, then use their education to gain entree into circles where they find new victims.

More commonly, delinquent youngsters use the classroom as an arena for criminal activity by fighting, lying, stealing, and engaging in power plays against teachers and other pupils. Basically, for them, school is boring, its requirements stupid, the subjects meaningless. Just as the criminal rejects his parents, he does the same to his teachers. It is neither incompetent teachers nor an irrelevant curriculum that drives him out. In fact, the school may offer him an individually tailored program, but no matter what he is offered, it does not suit him. Finally, he is expelled for disruptive behavior or grows so bored that he quits.

The notion that people become criminals because they are shut out of the job market is an absurdity. In the first place, most unemployed people are not criminals. More to the point, perhaps, is that many criminals do not want to work. They may complain that without skills they can't find employment. (Of course, it was their choice not to remain in school to acquire those skills.) But, as many a probation officer will observe, usually jobs of some sort are available, but criminals find them too menial and beneath them.

Some criminals are highly educated and successful at their work. Their very success may serve as a cover for crime. If a person has a solid work record, he is generally regarded as responsible and stable. But even legitimately acquired money, recognition, and power are not sufficient incentives for a criminal to live within the law. The point is that what a person's environment offers or lacks is not decisive in his becoming a criminal.

The public often criticizes the media for making crime enticing by glorifying both specific crimes and criminals. There has long been intense concern about the high incidence of violence in television programs that reach children. In the aftermath of school shootings during the 1990s, television again came under scrutiny for its effect on children. One highly publicized study released in 2000 claimed to support the contention that television causes aggression. But millions of people who frequently watch violence on television dramas, films, documentaries, and newscasts do not enact what they see.

A person already thinking about committing crimes may pick up ideas from the media, or become more confident about the feasibility of a particular crime. Fascinated and excited by the prospect of imitating and getting away with what he has watched on television or in a movie, he perpetrates what has come to be called a "copycat crime." Critical, though, is not what plays on the screen but what lies in the mind of the viewer. Television, movies, video games, magazines, or books will not turn a responsible person into a criminal. To believe otherwise is again to subscribe to the erroneous premise that external events easily shape human character.

4

Violent People Should Be Treated as Criminals Rather Than as Patients

Peter Breggin

Peter Breggin has been called "the conscience of psychiatry" for his efforts to reform the mental health field, including his promotion of psychotherapeutic approaches and his opposition to the escalating use of psychiatric medications. He often acts as a medical expert in criminal, malpractice, and product liability suits and is the author of many scientific articles and books.

Virginia Tech mass murderer Seung-Hui Cho was a disturbed mental patient who received frequent and varied psychiatric treatment, to no avail. The answer to dealing with violence in the mentally ill goes beyond psychiatric evaluations, hospitalization, and even drugs. The police and law enforcement should treat potentially dangerous people as criminals rather than patients. There is a real need to enforce security on college campuses and react quickly to lesser acts of violence before they escalate.

Focusing on Virginia Tech mass murderer [Seung-Hui] Cho as a disturbed mental patient has led media analysts to ponder how he could have been more readily identified by the mental health system. But Cho is not someone who slipped beneath the psychiatric radar. Instead, he was frequently detected as a large object on the screen. On separate occasions,

Peter Breggin, "The Real 'Mental Health Lesson' from Virginia Tech," *The Huffington Post*, April 19, 2007. Reproduced by permission.

he was involuntarily hospitalized, sent for psychological evaluation, and referred to the university counseling center. Consistent with getting him more psychiatric "help," experts have also opined on how he might have benefited from medication. These are all the wrong lessons.

The mental health system was fully alert to Cho's existence and to serious manifestations of dangerous behavior. A faculty member of the English department was so frightened by Cho's behavior that she insisted on having him pulled out of class. The police and the counseling center were notified and ultimately Cho was given individual tutoring, instead of quick removal from the campus. Also, a number of students called the campus police, probably at least twice in regard to his stalking behavior. Furthermore, he had previously been involuntarily hospitalized in Virginia as a danger to himself and others.

The answer to vengeful, violent people is not more mental health screening or more potent mental health interventions. Reliance on the whole range of this system from counseling to involuntary treatment failed. There is not a shred of scientific evidence that locking people up against their will or otherwise "treating" them reduces violence. As we'll see, quite the opposite is true.

So what was needed? Police intervention. Almost certainly, the police were hampered in taking appropriate actions by being encouraged to view Cho as a potential psychiatric patient rather than as a perpetrator. It's not politically correct to bring criminal charges against someone who is "mentally ill" and it's not politically correct to prosecute him or to remove him from the campus. Yet that's what was needed to protect the students. Two known episodes of stalking, setting a fire, and his threatening behavior in class should have been more than enough for the university administration to bring charges against him and to send him off campus.

Police need to be encouraged and empowered to treat potentially dangerous people more as criminals than as patients.

In particular, men stalking women should be handled as definitively as any perpetrator of hate crimes. Regardless of whether the victims want to press charges, the police should. Cho shouldn't have been allowed to get away with it a second time.

How would a police action have affected Cho? Would it have humiliated him and made him more violent? There's no way to have certainty about this, but anyone with experience dealing with threatening people knows that a good dose of "reality," a confrontation with the law, is much more of a wake-up call and a deterrent than therapeutic coddling. Furthermore, involuntary psychiatric treatment is one of the more humiliating experiences in American society, and tends to make people more angry, not less.

Instead of offering the promise of reducing violence, all psychiatric drugs carry the potential risk of driving the individual into violent madness.

The Effectiveness of Mental Health Interventions

Mental health interventions do not protect society because the person is almost always quickly discharged because his insurance coverage has run out or because mental health professionals, who as a group have no particular capacity to make such determinations, will decide that the patient is no longer a danger to himself or others. Indeed, in December 2005, when the university obtained a temporary detention order against Cho, a magistrate referred him for a mental health evaluation that found "his insight and judgment are normal." Need I say more about the hazards of relying on mental health screening and evaluation to identify dangerous perpetrators—even after they have already been threatening people?

Psychiatry's last resort for presumably violent people is involuntary hospitalization. Not only does it almost always lead to rapid release, it does not help the involuntary patient. Coerced treatment is not perceived or experienced as "helpful" by the recipient but as unjust bullying. If coercion accomplishes anything, it teaches the "patient" to stay far away from all providers of mental health services.

And what about drugs for the treatment of violence? The FDA [Food and Drug Administration] has not approved any medications for the control of violence because there are no such medications. Yes, it is possible to temporarily immobilize mind and body alike with a shot of an "antipsychotic" drug like Haldol; but that only works as long as the person is virtually paralyzed and confined—and forced drugging invariably breeds more resentment.

Instead of offering the promise of reducing violence, all psychiatric drugs carry the potential risk of driving the individual into violent madness. For example, both the newer antidepressants such as Prozac, Paxil, Zoloft and Celexa, and the antipsychotic drugs such as Risperdal and Zyprexa, cause a disorder caused akathisia—a terrible inner sensation of agitation accompanied by a compulsion to move about. Akathisia is known to drive people to suicide and to aggression. Indeed, these tragic outcomes of drug-induced akathisia are so well documented that they are described in the most establishment psychiatric book of all, the American Psychiatric Association's *Diagnostic and Statistical Manual of Mental Disorders* (DSM).

The Negative Effect of Drugs

For the past fifteen years or more, I've been writing about the capacity of psychiatric drugs to cause mayhem, murder and suicide. In early 2005 the FDA finally issued a warning that antidepressants cause both suicidality and violence. For example, the FDA's new mandated warning label for antidepressants states that these drugs produce "anxiety, agitation, panic attacks, insomnia, irritability, hostility, aggressiveness, impulsivity, akathisia (psychomotor restlessness), hypomania, and mania."

Note the reference to "irritability, hostility, aggressiveness, impulsivity" in the label or package insert for antidepressants. That's a formula for violence. Note the mention of akathisia, another source of both violence and suicide. And finally, note the reference to mania, yet another drug-induced syndrome associated with violence and suicide.

The violent rampage [at Virginia Tech] should confirm that psychiatric interventions don't prevent violence and instead they can cause it.

As a psychiatrist and medical expert, I have personally evaluated dozens of cases of individuals driven to violence by psychiatric drugs of every type, but most commonly the newer antidepressants. One of the cases I evaluated, the Columbine shooter Eric Harris, looks the most like Cho. Both were very emotionally disturbed in an extremely violent fashion for a prolonged period of time. For the entire year that Eric Harris was evolving his manic-like violence, he was taking Luvox, a drug known to cause mania at a high rate in young people.

In my book *Reclaiming Our Children*, I analyzed the clinical and scientific reasons for believing that Eric Harris's violence was caused by prescribed Luvox and I've also testified to the same under oath in deposition in a case related to Columbine. In my book the *Antidepressant Fact Book*, I also warned that stopping antidepressants can be as dangerous as starting them, since they can cause very disturbing and painful withdrawal reactions.

We have not been informed whether or not Cho was taking psychiatric drugs at the time he unleashed his violence; but even if he wasn't, he might have been tipped over into violent madness weeks or months earlier by a drug like Prozac,

Paxil, or Zoloft. He could also have been undergoing severe drug withdrawal. *Investigators should set a set a high priority on obtaining and publishing Cho's psychiatric drug history.*

To focus on Cho as a "mental patient" or "schizophrenic" distracts from the real need to enforce security on college campuses, or in any setting, by reacting definitively to lesser acts of violence before they escalate. It also maligns people with serious mental problems, the vast majority who are, above else, inoffensive and overly docile.

Stop Violence by Confronting It

The violence unleashed on the Virginia Tech campus should not lead to calls for more mental health screening, more mental health interventions, or more drugs. Instead, the violent rampage should confirm that psychiatric interventions don't prevent violence and instead they can cause it. Early on, Cho should have been confronted by the police and by university administrators with the reality that his behavior was unacceptable and he should have been suspended. In other words, he should have been treated as a criminal who was stalking women, and as an obviously threatening individual, not as a potential mental patient. These measures might have confronted him with sufficient reality to nip his violence in the bud and more certainly would have removed him from the circumstances that he found intolerably stimulating, while also removing him from so many targets of opportunity.

5

The Mentally Ill Are Kept in Prisons Due to Inadequate Health Services

William Kanapaux

William Kanapaux is a reporter for Psychiatric Times, *a monthly periodical featuring clinical news and special reports.*

Due to inadequate mental health services, prisons are used as a warehouse for the mentally ill. Prisons hold three times more people with mental illness than do psychiatric hospitals, putting a strain on housing resources as well as failing to address the distinctive needs of the prisoners themselves. The symptoms of mental illness are often seen as disruptive and can lead to arrest and to punishments that exacerbate the condition of mentally ill prisoners. As yet, there has been no effective policy response to keep the mentally ill out of the criminal justice system.

On any given day, it is estimated that about 70,000 inmates in U.S. prisons are psychotic. Anywhere from 200,000 to 300,000 male and female prison inmates suffer from mental disorders such as schizophrenia, bipolar disorder and major depression. Prisons hold three times more people with mental illness than do psychiatric hospitals, and U.S. prisoners have rates of mental illness that are up to four times greater than rates for the general population.

These are the findings of a report by Human Rights Watch, released Oct. 22, 2003. Many of the statistics cited by the or-

William Kanapaux, "Guilty of Mental Illness," *Psychiatric Times*, vol. 21, no. 1, January 1, 2004. Reproduced by permission.

ganization have been released by various organizations and agencies, but the 215-page report provides a more complete picture of the U.S. prison system as the nation's primary mental health care facilities. . . .

> The factors that contribute to a person being in jail in the first place relate to inadequate access to quality behavioral health services.

"Ill Equipped: U.S. Prisons and Offenders with Mental Illness" resulted from two years of research and hundreds of interviews with mental health care experts, prisoners, correction officials and attorneys. It reported that few prisons offer adequate mental health care services and that the prison environment is dangerous and debilitating for prisoners who have mental illness. These prisoners are victimized by other inmates, punished by prison staff for behaviors associated with their illnesses and often placed in highly restrictive cells that exacerbate their symptoms.

The U.S. prison system is "not only serving as a warehouse for the mentally ill, but, by relying on extremely restrictive housing for mentally ill prisoners, it is acting as an incubator for worse illness and psychiatric breakdowns," according to the report.

Factors Leading to Incarceration

The high prevalence of mental illness in the criminal justice system is related to several factors that psychiatrists should care about, Fred Osher, M.D., director of the Center for Behavioral Health, Justice and Pubic Policy at the University of Maryland, told *Psychiatric Times* [*PT*].

The factors that contribute to a person being in jail in the first place relate to inadequate access to quality behavioral health services, Osher told *PT*. Without these services, people with mental illnesses often engage in behaviors that capture the attention of law enforcement and lead to arrests.

The majority of people with mental illness in the criminal justice system are there for misdemeanors and crimes of survival, according to Osher. He said, "There's a whole host of folks who land in the criminal justice system because of their behavioral disorders." The problem primarily affects people on the margins of society. They are often minorities, almost always impoverished and disabled by their illness.

Inmates with mental illness are often punished for their symptoms.

The federal government's war on drugs has swept up people with mental illness at higher rates than those for the general population because more people with mental illness use and abuse drugs, Osher said. He added, "I think we want to watch the policy around punishment versus treatment, and we want to be advocates for treatment first."

There is also a high prevalence of people coming into the mental health care system with a history of involvement with criminal justice. Mental health care professionals need to be aware of this and think about the necessary communications with law enforcement and correctional supervision officials. "I think the issue is that many folks in mental health care don't want to work with people who have a criminal justice history, but they do anyway," Osher said. "They're just not looking for it."

The general consensus with the criminal justice system is that people with serious mental illness should not be there. It is a bad situation for both the prisoners and the facilities.

"We hear that everywhere," Chris Koyanagi, policy director at the Washington, D.C.-based Bazelon Center for Mental

Health Law, told *PT.* "From jails all over the country, from prison administrators, from senior correctional administrators."

Chronically underfunded, the existing mental health system today does not reach and provide mental health treatment to anywhere near the number of people who need it.

Inmates with mental illness are often punished for their symptoms. Being disruptive, refusing to obey orders, and engaging in acts of self-mutilation and attempted suicide can all result in punitive action. As a result, the report noted, prisoners with mental illness often have extensive disciplinary histories.

Frequently, the prisoners end up in isolation units. "In the most extreme cases, conditions are truly horrific," the report, stated, adding:

> Mentally ill prisoners locked in segregation with no treatment at all; confined in filthy and beastly hot cells; left for days covered in feces they have smeared over their bodies; taunted, abused, or ignored by prison staff; given so little water during summer heat waves that they drink from their toilet bowls. . . . Suicidal prisoners are left naked and unattended for days on end in barren, cold observation cells. Poorly trained correctional officers have accidentally asphyxiated mentally ill prisoners whom they were trying to restrain.

Root Causes

The report found that the high incarceration rate for people with mental illness is a direct result of underfunded and fragmented services. "Chronically underfunded, the existing mental health system today does not reach and provide mental health treatment to anywhere near the number of people who need it," it explained.

Public mental health care systems are stretched for money, according to Koyanagi. And they have people within their priority population who demand services and are responsive to less expensive treatments. "Those folks tend to get their needs met," she said.

People with serious mental illness who are left out of services are more difficult to reach and more difficult to treat because of the nature of their illnesses, she said. They may be dually diagnosed or already homeless.

Koyanagi noted that, from a cynical perspective, it can be said that criminalization is to the advantage of public mental health care systems. "The system can pretend they're not there."

When these individuals do leave the criminal justice system, they often can't get into local community mental health care programs, just as they can't get into public housing. "They're deemed unsuitable for that particular program because of their record," she said.

People who are visibly homeless or have drug and alcohol problems are landing in jails and prisons with greater frequency.

Prison Populations

Over the last several decades, states have emptied their psychiatric hospitals without moving sufficient resources into community-based programs. Meanwhile, overall prison populations have soared.

It is tempting for people to conclude that a causal relationship exists between the decreased number of people in state psychiatric hospitals and the increased number of inmates with mental illness, Osher said, but the data do not support that belief.

Over the last 20 years, the U.S. prison population has experienced an enormous increase, with about 3% of the adult population now under some form of jail or correctional supervision, he said. Consequently, the problem has more to do with the way that people get arrested. People who are visibly homeless or have drug and alcohol problems are landing in jails and prisons with greater frequency.

The jails themselves represent a public health opportunity, according to Osher. Given estimates that about 15% to 17% of people coming into jails have a serious mental illness and that there are 11 million arrests a year, "that's a huge number of folks who are mostly not connected with systems of care." Screening programs could help identify those people so that they can get connected with appropriate treatment programs.

People who are privately insured are not immune from run-ins with the criminal justice system. A privately insured person with bipolar disorder can run into serious problems during a manic episode. In such cases, encounters with the legal system are usually less harmful, Koyanagi said. Often these individuals can be stabilized and returned to services within the community.

The people who tend to get stuck in the criminal justice system usually have long records, she told *PT*. "It doesn't just happen once, it happens again and again because nothing is done to deal with the underlying problems. And you end up in prison because you have a long rap sheet."

Koyanagi agreed that drug crimes are a major contributor to the growing number of mentally ill in jails and prisons. Whether a user or a seller, people with co-occurring mental illness and substance abuse get swept up by punitive drug penalties, she said.

Efforts to Respond

Koyanagi and Osher both served on the steering committee for the Criminal Justice/Mental Health Consensus Project report, which was issued in 2002. The project represented an unprecedented national effort to bring together federal policymakers with criminal justice and mental health care professionals to create a more responsive system for addressing the needs of people with mental illness who are at risk of involvement or are already involved with the criminal justice system.

Jail and prison overcrowding issues are high on the priority lists of wardens and sheriffs in this country, and correction officials are clamoring for improved mental health treatment in communities to deal with this, Osher said. Because of the high rates of people with serious mental illness in the criminal justice system and the problems they create in terms of service utilization and jail management, the mental health care field has partners in law enforcement and the courts and among corrections personnel.

"When you go before a state legislature and advocate for better mental health services as a psychiatrist, it seems self-serving," Osher said. "But when you go before them as a warden or a sheriff or a police officer, folks listen."

The first recommendation in the Human Rights Watch report, which drew upon the work of the Consensus Project, is for enactment of the Mentally Ill Offender Treatment and Crime Reduction Act, which was introduced in 2003 by Sen. Mike DeWine (R-Ohio). On Oct. 29, 2003, the U.S. Senate unanimously passed the bill, which would provide five-year grants to states and localities that could be used for mental health courts, in-jail treatment, transitional services and training. The bill now awaits action in the House, where it was introduced by Rep. Ted Strickland (D-Ohio) [the act was signed into law October 30, 2004].

How to Respond

The Bazelon Center is concerned that if the bill passes, the money will be spent to build up mental health services within jails and prisons without focusing on community-based services that would keep people out of the criminal justice system in the first place, Koyanagi said. Nothing in the bill prevents the money being used primarily or exclusively for services in jails and prisons, she said. The Bazelon Center feels that services in these facilities should be the responsibility of criminal justice agencies.

Mental health care systems need to develop evidence-based services such as assertive community treatment, which takes an intensive team approach to helping a person receive treatment and supports, and integrated substance abuse services, Koyanagi said. While funding services within the criminal justice system deals with the immediate problem of what to do with a prisoner who is psychotic, it is a temporary, not a systemic, solution.

"The ultimate goal of people in the criminal justice system is not to have so many of these folks in their facilities," Koyanagi said. "Building up mental health services inside of jails and prisons doesn't encourage judges not to put people there."

A judge may see that someone is not being helped by the community mental health care system and decide that, in jail, that person might be diagnosed, put on the right medications and get better.

"Judges have told us they do that," Koyanagi told *PT*. However, prisons and jails are not therapeutic environments, and serving time gives a person a record that follows them throughout life.

As of yet, there hasn't been an effective policy response to the problem of keeping people with mental illness out of jails and prisons, Koyanagi said. She added, "If that continues to be true, there may be more and more litigation against both criminal justice agencies and possibly mental health agencies, too."

6

Psychiatric Hospitals Are Not Equivalent to Prisons

Joanmarie Ilaria Davoli

Joanmarie Ilaria Davoli is an associate professor of law at Florida Coastal School of Law.

Psychiatric hospitals should not be equated with prisons. Psychiatric hospitals are staffed with specialized professionals whose focus is treatment whereas prisons are staffed with guards meant to enforce time served as punishment. The disappearance of psychiatric hospitals has forced the mentally ill into prisons, which are not equipped to handle their needs. The insanity defense remains a viable option in criminal proceedings but should be considered on a case-by-case basis.

Despite its acceptance in criminal law theory, the insanity defense remains controversial. Endless books, television shows, and movies continue to depict crafty murderers "faking crazy" to avoid conviction. In addition, the insanity defense remains unpopular with defense attorneys, and is typically only asserted in serious cases. Although the insanity defense is rarely used, a large number of individuals currently incarcerated suffer from serious mental illnesses, and were mentally ill at the time of their convictions. Typically, the mental illnesses of these defendants were never considered during trial or sentencing.

There exists a strong prevailing belief that successful use of the insanity defense results in criminal defendants being "sub-

Joanmarie Ilaria Davoli, "Reconsidering the Consequences of an Insanity Acquittal," *New England Journal on Criminal and Civil Confinement*, vol. 31, no. 1, Winter 2005, pp. 3–14. Reproduced by permission.

sequently incarcerated in maximum security institutions for periods of time as long as, or, in many cases, much longer than they would have spent in prison for the same offense" [according to researcher Michael Perlin]. In years past, insanity acquittees were often hospitalized for an amount of time in excess of their potential criminal sentence had there been a conviction. However, on-going revisions to the criminal codes combined with more effective treatments for mental illness have altered the consequences of an insanity verdict.

There has also been the assumption that time spent in a psychiatric hospital is equivalent to or even worse than confinement in prison. This assumption has typically been unchallenged by legal scholars. For many years, confinement in mental hospitals has been equated with imprisonment. This confinement has been without regard to differences in location, atmosphere, physical surroundings, personnel, levels of privacy, and daily experiences of the individuals confined to each. Scholarly writings continue to portray psychiatric treatment as just another term for "prison sentence"—implying that an individual is "serving time" for being mentally ill. Such negative stereotypes of psychiatric hospitalization contribute to defense counsel's reluctance to advise clients to assert the insanity defense.

This article will examine the outdated assumption that criminal defendants who successfully raise the insanity defense remain unjustly confined in psychiatric hospitals long past any medically necessary time period. Using the illustration of a modern insanity case, *Commonwealth v. Bobbitt*, this article will detail the procedures used in the Commonwealth of Virginia following a not guilty by reason of insanity verdict. The article will further question the contention that psychiatric hospitals are equivalent to or worse than prisons, and that individuals acquitted by reasons of insanity are "sentenced" to a lifetime of psychiatric hospitalization. Finally, the article will suggest that defense attorneys should consider creative approaches to addressing a defendant's mental illness during representation on a criminal charge.

Commonwealth v. Lorena Bobbitt

On June 23, 1993, Lorena Bobbitt used a twelve-inch kitchen knife to sever her husband's penis, fled from her apartment, and threw his penis into a nearby field. Her husband's "penis, which was retrieved by rescue workers from the field where Lorena Bobbitt threw it, was reattached by two surgeons in a 9½-hour operation" [according to writer Patricia Davis]. Lorena Bobbitt was subsequently charged with malicious wounding of her husband.

At trial, Lorena Bobbitt asserted the insanity defense and presented evidence that she suffered from depression, post-traumatic stress disorder, and battered women's syndrome that resulted from numerous beatings and other abuse at the hands of her husband. "More than four dozen witnesses gave accounts of instances in which John Bobbitt, a former Marine and nightclub bouncer, had beaten, punched, kicked and choked his wife" [according to writer Carlos Sanchez]. Psychiatrists for both the defense and the prosecution "agreed that Lorena Bobbitt had been battered throughout the couple's four and a half-year marriage and that she had been raped just before the cutting" [Davis wrote]. The experts further testified that Bobbitt was [according to writer Lorraine Adams] "severely depressed and suffered from post-traumatic stress disorder. So there was evidence of mental disease."

However, the experts disagreed as to whether or not the mental disease produced an irresistible impulse in Lorena Bobbitt, necessary for a finding of insanity. "A defense psychiatrist, Susan J. Fiester, testified that mental disease led Bobbitt to cut off her husband's penis," [wrote Adams] supporting the insanity claim. However, the prosecution experts [noted Sanchez] "stopped short of concluding that she broke from reality that morning and was unable to control her impulse to cut him." The jury agreed with the defense expert, and Lorena Bobbitt was found not guilty by reason of insanity on January 21, 1994.

Lorena Bobbitt was hospitalized for only forty-five days, a mere fraction of the potential twenty-year prison sentence she risked if convicted of malicious wounding.

Most significant, for purposes of this article, are the procedures that followed her insanity acquittal. As a result of her acquittal by reason of insanity, Lorena Bobbitt was automatically transferred to the custody of the Commissioner of Mental Health pursuant to Virginia Code Section 19.2-182.2. During the statutorily mandated forty-five-day observation and diagnosis period, she was evaluated [according to the law] "as to whether the she may be released with or without commitment, or require commitment." The state hospital experts then drafted reports that could have included any of the following three recommendations: that Lorena Bobbitt "was a danger to herself and the community and should remain confined, that she be released without condition, or that she be released into an outpatient treatment program."

In February of 1994, the presiding judge from the criminal trial held a civil commitment hearing to review Lorena Bobbitt's current mental health and treatment needs. At that hearing, the court considered reports from the psychiatric hospital as to her current state of psychiatric health, and need for hospitalization. The judge found that Lorena Bobbitt did not pose a threat to herself or the community, and [according to writers Marylou Tousignant and Sanchez] "ordered the 24-year-old manicurist released from a Virginia state mental hospital, provided she gets weekly outpatient therapy and does not leave the state without permission."

The significance of the Lorena Bobbitt case is that her insanity acquittal did *not* result in the ubiquitous and dire prediction that she would spend her life in a psychiatric hospital if she were successful in her defense. Not only was she released from the hospital after the forty-five-day evaluation, but she was eventually released from outpatient commitment. Thus, instead of spending more time in the hospital than her potential sentence would have otherwise required had she been convicted, the exact opposite occurred. Lorena Bobbitt was hospitalized for only forty-five days, a mere fraction of the potential twenty-year prison sentence she risked if convicted of malicious wounding.

The Virginia procedure for post-acquittal treatment in an insanity case, often described as particularly harsh, requires confinement of an insanity acquittee *only* for a period of time sufficient to diagnose the illness, determine the prognosis, and treat the patient's illness. Despite dire predictions, there were no conniving attempts by demented hospital staff to force frightening treatments on Lorena Bobbitt; no power-craving doctors tried to assert complete control over her; and no grant-seeking hospital director conspired to keep up the number of hospital beds by keeping her against her will. In short, the post-acquittal statutory procedure in Virginia ensured that individuals who are *not* in need of psychiatric care are *not* left to languish in the hospital. Instead, the law protected Lorena Bobbitt's due process rights while also considering the Commonwealth of Virginia's interest in public safety.

The goal of psychiatric hospitalization is to provide care and treatment, not to punish.

Not Guilty by Reason of Insanity

Insanity acquittees in Virginia are not automatically or necessarily locked up in the back wards of forgotten psychiatric warehouses. As was seen in the Bobbitt case, Virginia provides a statutory scheme designed to require hospitalization for individuals who are currently ill, in need of treatment, and potentially dangerous to self or the community. The Commonwealth of Virginia does not arbitrarily lock up all insanity acquittees for indefinite time periods.

While the procedures detailed above in the Bobbitt case were previously followed for all insanity acquittees in Virginia, public outcry about the fate of misdemeanor acquittees prompted recent revisions to the Virginia Code. In 2001, the Virginia State Crime Commission issued a report critical of the length of time misdemeanor offenders acquitted by reason of insanity were hospitalized. As a result, the Virginia Code was amended to limit the amount of time an individual could be held involuntarily in a psychiatric hospital as a result of being found not guilty of a misdemeanor by reason of insanity.

Virginia Code Section 19.2-182.5 states that "An acquittee who is found not guilty of a misdemeanor by reason of insanity on or after July 1, 2002, shall remain in the custody of the Commissioner . . . for a period not to exceed one year from the date of acquittal." The majority of jailable misdemeanor offenses in Virginia carry a maximum one-year sentence. Thus, the revised statute effectively matches the time a misdemeanor acquittee can be held involuntarily in a psychiatric hospital to the maximum criminal sentence he could have received if convicted of the underlying offense.

These new procedures essentially eliminate the risk that a defendant will be penalized by lengthy confinement if he asserts the insanity defense. However, by matching possible time in a hospital to that of the potential criminal sentence, this law once again equates psychiatric hospitalization with imprisonment. Instead of accepting that equation as legitimate, the legislators should have considered a medically based standard to determine the need for psychiatric hospitalization, such as the requirements of the patient and the severity of the illness.

Psychiatric Hospital vs. Prison

When an individual suffers from a serious mental illness and commits a crime as a result of that illness, going to a psychiatric hospital for care and treatment is far more appropriate than receiving a prison sentence. The goal of psychiatric hospitalization is to provide care and treatment, not to punish. Psychiatric hospitals are just that, hospitals. While seemingly self-evident, this is nevertheless an important and often overlooked distinction. Prisons are designed to punish individuals who commit crimes. . . .

The atmosphere, activities and purpose of psychiatric hospitals differ from the prison environment. In addition, hospital staff are specially trained to provide treatment and care for psychiatric patients.

An individual suffering from serious mental illness finds adjusting to prison extremely difficult. . . .

Prisons and jail guards are trained to maintain order and enforce punishments. They are not trained or equipped to respond to individuals suffering from severe mental illness.

Examples of the mistreatment of the incarcerated mentally ill are plentiful. A 1994 report on the conditions of mentally ill prisoners in Ohio led a local newspaper to describe the report "as reading like a Charles Dickens novel: tales of naked men and women languishing in fetid cells, sometimes without heat or hot water, or being punished for behavior that appears to be entirely the result of their mental illness." Prisons are simply not designed to provide psychiatric care and treatment to mentally ill individuals.

The opposite is also true. Psychiatric hospitals cannot be expected to function as prisons. Although the history of psychiatric hospitals in the United States has included instances of abuse, neglect and substandard facilities, such treatment is not the goal or standard of psychiatric hospitals. "The state hospitals have been often maligned, but they did fill a vital need. Even with the best community support system, there are individuals who need an asylum" [according to Ralph Slovenko].

Whether or not to raise the insanity defense should be an informed decision, made on the basis of reason and relevant information, not because anti-psychiatry myths left over from the 1960s and 1970s continue to dominate the attitudes of the criminal defense bar.

Unlike a prison sentence that imposes a specific punishment as a result of specific criminal behavior, time spent in a psychiatric hospital is determined by the illness and treatment needs of the individual, not the amount of time needed or deserved for punishment. An individual may spend ten years in a hospital because that individual is profoundly mentally ill and is incapable of functioning outside a hospital setting.

Throughout the history of the United States, there have been instances of abuse in both systems, and attempts to reform them. However, the forty-year campaign to abolish psychiatric hospitals has nearly been achieved without establishing effective new venues in which extremely ill individuals receive appropriate care. Unfortunately, abolishing psychiatric hospitals does not eliminate suffering or illness, although it does result in increased numbers of mentally ill individuals incarcerated in prisons.

Thus, in discussing possible outcomes with a client, defense counsel should not naively advise a client that confinement in prison and confinement in psychiatric hospitals are equivalent. Instead, defense counsel should first become educated on the condition of the various psychiatric hospitals within the state as well as the conditions under which the mentally ill are incarcerated. Decisions and advice based on knowledge and accurate information will result in better representation of the client, and better serve the client's interests.

Raising the Insanity Defense

Individuals suffering from serious mental illnesses that cause them to commit crimes should not be discouraged from raising the insanity defense because of outdated myths and irrational fears on the part of defense counsel. Instead, criminal defendants should be informed of all the facts relevant to the insanity acquittee procedure within their jurisdiction, the type of hospitalization available, the conditions of those hospitals, and the likelihood of the various verdicts. Whether or not to raise the insanity defense should be an informed decision, made on the basis of reason and relevant information, not because anti-psychiatry myths left over from the 1960s and 1970s continue to dominate the attitudes of the criminal defense bar. Additionally, when representing an individual who suffers from a serious mental illness, defense counsel should research and explore alternatives to prosecution. Counsel should also consider creatively introducing mental illness issues in arguments for mitigation of the client's sentence.

7

The Mentally Ill Are Mishandled by the Justice System

American Civil Liberties Union

The American Civil Liberties Union (ACLU) is a nonprofit organization that works to defend and preserve individual rights and liberties. The ACLU provides legal assistance in cases where the organization considers civil liberties to be at risk and also lobbies legislators.

Close to 300,000 inmates in prison or jail are mentally ill. Mentally ill people on trial must meet the legal definition of insanity to decrease responsibility for their crimes. There is a fundamental lack of due process for the mentally ill that violates international human rights standards. The death penalty should be suspended for all mentally ill prisoners.

Mental illness is defined as "Any of various conditions characterized by impairment of an individual's normal cognitive, emotional, or behavioral functioning, and caused by social, psychological, biochemical, genetic, or other factors, such as infection or head trauma." Some of the more common illnesses experienced by inmates on death row may include:

- Bipolar Disorder

- Borderline Personality Disorder

- Post-Traumatic Stress Disorder

American Civil Liberties Union, "Mental Illness and the Death Penalty in the United States," ACLU, January 31, 2005. Reproduced by permission.

- Schizoaffective Disorder

- Schizophrenia

- Depression

- Recurrent Thoughts of Death or Suicide

Over 60 people diagnosed as mentally ill or with mental retardation have been executed in the United States since 1983. While precise statistics are not available, it is estimated that 5 to 10 percent of people on death row have a serious mental illness.

Psychotic Symptoms Common on Death Row

After evaluating dozens of death row inmates, Dr. Dorothy Otnow Lewis, a professor of psychiatry at New York University, found that almost without fail they all had damaged brains due to illness or trauma, and most were also victims of vicious beatings and sexual abuse as children. She found psychotic symptoms, especially paranoia, to be common on death row.

A person's mental illness affects every stage of passage through the criminal justice system.

Similarly grim figures were reported by the Bureau of Justice Statistics:

- In 1998, an estimated 283,000 mentally ill offenders were incarcerated in prison or jail.

- Over 30 percent of male mentally ill inmates and 78 percent of female mentally ill inmates reported physical or sexual abuse.

- Mentally ill state prison inmates were also more than twice as likely as other inmates to report living on the street or in a shelter in the 12 months prior to arrest (20 compared to 9 percent).

What's more, according to many mental health experts, these statistics may underestimate the problem of the incarceration of the mentally ill due to under-reporting by people who might not want to disclose the information or are unaware of their illness.

The 1986 Supreme Court decision *Ford v. Wainwright* ruled that the execution of the insane violates the Eighth Amendment's ban on cruel and unusual punishment. *Ford* only prohibits the execution of a person who does not understand the reason for, or the reality of, his or her punishment. Tragically, many people who are mentally ill do not qualify as being insane, resulting in severely mentally incompetent people being executed regularly. Thus, *Ford* has provided only minimal protection and has not prevented the executions of seriously mentally ill prisoners.

In death penalty cases, the issue of mental illness can be raised as a mitigating factor.

Popular misconceptions about mental illness are partially responsible for the railroading of mentally ill persons through the criminal justice system. From arrest to the determination of competency to stand trial and beyond, a person's mental illness affects every stage of passage through the criminal justice system.

Behavior associated with mental illness is often perceived as bizarre and suspicious, thus drawing police attention, even if the person has not committed a crime. Untrained to recognize and handle mental illness, arresting officers and other staff inappropriately assume the arrestee understands such things as their Miranda rights. Mentally ill people are more likely to give a false confession, especially if they are delusional.

Mentally Ill People and Culpability

The concept of culpability [responsibility] is an important aspect of who is sentenced to death. Culpability signifies qualities such as consciousness, reason, and responsibility. It is precisely these qualities that are disabled and distorted by mental illness, and therefore a gap exists between a mentally ill offender's behavior and his culpability.

In death penalty cases, the issue of mental illness can be raised as a mitigating factor. Mitigating factors are particular circumstances that are legally recognized to decrease a defendant's culpability and result in a non–death penalty sentence. Since untreated brain disorders can cause individuals to act in inappropriate or criminal ways, certain aspects of mental illness, such as a defendant's diminished capacity to appreciate the criminality of his conduct, and to conform his conduct to the requirements of the law, are codified as mitigating factors in capital cases. In a majority of cases, dangerous or violent behavior exhibited by persons with brain disorders is the result of neglect, and inappropriate, or insufficient treatment, of their illness. Therefore, mentally ill offenders are by definition not the worst of the worst offenders.

At the trial stage, research has shown that jurors often misunderstand the relationship between mental illness and mitigating factors, and that they are prone to mistakenly treat mental illness as an aggravating factor and sentence the person to death. For example, one study found a positive correlation between the jurors' consideration of the (mitigating) factor "extreme mental or emotional disturbance" and the imposition of death sentences. Another study revealed jurors wrongly interpreted instructions on "future dangerousness" to mean the death penalty was mandatory for mentally ill defendants.

Misinformed perceptions of mental illness by jurors affect their decisions. When police officers, prosecutors, judges, and jurors act upon these misinformed perceptions and misunderstand the relevance of mental illness to a defendant's culpability, the mentally ill person is likely to be wrongfully convicted or sentenced to death.

Mentally ill people have been and continue to be executed in the United States in clear violation of . . . international standards.

International Human Rights Standards

International law prohibits the execution of the mentally ill, and almost every country in the world has outlawed such executions.

- The United Nations Safeguards Guaranteeing Protection of the Rights of Those Facing the Death Penalty, adopted in 1984, states "nor shall the death sentence be carried out on persons who have become insane."

- In 1997, the U.N. Special Rapporteur on Extrajudicial, Summary or Arbitrary Executions called upon these governments that use the death penalty "with respect to minors and the mentally ill to bring their domestic legislation into conformity with international legal standards."

- And in 2000, the U.N. Commission on Human Rights urged states that maintain the death penalty "not to impose it on a person suffering from any form of mental disorder; not to execute any such person."

Mentally ill people have been and continue to be executed in the United States in clear violation of these international standards.

Domestic Laws Fail to Protect

While U.S. constitutional law is in line with some of the international standards outlined above, the number of mentally ill people sentenced to death and executed attests to the failures of the law to protect them. The American Bar Association has reported that "fundamental due process is systematically lacking" in the capital punishment structure, and that these systematic failures "tragically and irreparably" harm defendants in many capital cases.

In addition to the flawed application of the laws that handle mental illness and the death penalty, and the inadequate procedures states follow to diagnose and treat mentally ill inmates, there are also problems with the laws themselves and the way they do not account for the intricacies of mental illness with their narrow definitions of insanity.

Medicating to Execute

Narrow definitions of insanity leave room for manipulation by the state with an interest in executing prisoners. *Ford*'s minimal definition of insanity allows states to endorse the practice of forcibly medicating an inmate to the lowest point of competency legally required prior to his execution. The Supreme Court recognizes the very serious side effects of psychotropic drugs but maintains that a prisoner can be forcibly medicated if it's in his best medical interest, or if it is necessary for the state to control the inmate.

An example of medicating an inmate to make him eligible for execution is Charles Singleton. Singleton was executed by the state of Arkansas on January 6, 2004. He was a paranoid schizophrenic who suffered from psychotic symptoms such as "constant voices that speak of killing him." By the late 1980s he had begun to suffer delusions, such as that his cell was possessed by demons and that his thoughts were being stolen as he read the Bible. He described himself variously as the "Holy Ghost" and "God and the Supreme Court." He expressed the belief that execution was simply a matter of stopping his breathing, and that a judge could restart it again—clearly a lack of understanding of the nature of execution.

In 1997, prison authorities obtained a court order to forcibly medicate him to render him temporarily mentally competent, saying he posed a danger to himself and others, but conveniently rendering him eligible to be put to death.

Singleton's attorneys filed a lawsuit arguing the state could not constitutionally restore his client's mental competency through the use of forced medication and then execute him. In October 2001, a panel of the 8th U.S. Circuit Court of Appeals ruled that Singleton be sentenced to life in prison without the possibility of parole.

The state appealed, and in February 2004, a sharply divided full 8th Circuit Court lifted a stay of execution for Singleton. The court said at the time that because Singleton was "voluntarily taking his medication" and because Arkansas had an interest in having sane inmates, the side effect of sanity should not affect Singleton's sentence.

Other Examples of the Execution of the Mentally Ill

Kelsey Patterson was executed in Texas on May 18, 2004, for a double murder he committed in 1992. Patterson had a long history of serious mental illness. He was first diagnosed with paranoid schizophrenia in 1981, and his symptoms of hallucinations, delusions, paranoia, confused thinking, and altered senses, emotions, and behavior had been well documented.

A jury found Patterson competent to stand trial despite his behavior at the competency hearing and at his 1993 trial, even though he repeatedly interrupted proceedings with confused ramblings about his implanted devices and the elaborate conspiracy against him. These displays alone provided enough compelling evidence that he was delusional and incapable of understanding what was going on or being able to assist in his defense. Moreover, expert witnesses and several judges involved in Patterson's trial stated clearly that he undoubtedly suffered from paranoid schizophrenia. But despite Patterson's severe mental illness, as well as several egregious flaws in the trial, Patterson was still executed.

James Blake Colburn was executed by the state of Texas on March 26, 2003. Like Patterson, he was also a paranoid schizophrenic with a documented history of mental illness. In addition to schizophrenia, Colburn exhibited signs of post-traumatic stress disorder due to being raped as a teenager. Colburn had made several suicide attempts over the years and had a long history of drug abuse beginning in his adolescent years. At the time of the homicide, Colburn was "actively psychotic" and in his taped confession he stated that he had been "hearing voices telling him that this murder was a way for him to get back into prison."

Colburn's mental illness was even acknowledged by the trial prosecutor in his opening statement: "You are going to hear evidence that the defendant is a paranoid schizophrenic. . . . You will hear evidence that he's heard voices and you are going to see him on tape. He's shaking or fidgeting. The State is not going to contest or deny any of that. . . ." Despite this clear admission, the defense attorney did not ask for a competency hearing and the jury handed down a verdict of death.

Pernell Ford was executed by the state of Alabama on June 1, 2000, for the murders of two women during a 1983 burglary. Ford was 18 years old at the time of his conviction. From the age of six, Pernell Ford spent extended periods in mental health institutions, and by 13 was being prescribed powerful anti-psychotic and anti-depressant drugs. During his adolescence he attempted suicide several times, by methods including overdose, hanging and poisoning. He was also reported to have attempted suicide on death row.

Shortly before his trial, Ford dismissed his lawyers. He was found competent to act as his own lawyer despite his youth, his limited formal education, an IQ measured at 80, and his history of mental problems. The only "defense" he offered was that God would intervene at the trial and bring the victims back to life. For most of the proceedings, Pernell Ford remained silent and withdrawn. There was no opening statement on his behalf, no objections, and no cross-examination of any witnesses.

At his sentencing, Pernell Ford dressed himself in a white bed sheet, worn toga-style with a belt and shoulder strap made from a white towel. In a long speech, he asked the judge to have the coffins of the victims brought into the courtroom so that God could raise them from the dead in front of the jurors. After sentencing him to death, the judge told Ford that by law he would receive an automatic appeal. Pernell Ford responded that he did not want one.

Ford initially was set for execution in July 1999, but a federal appeals court delayed his death after his former attorney questioned his mental state. At a court hearing, Ford testified he could leave death row through "translation," and had visited heaven and other spots worldwide while in prison. He said he had millions of dollars in a Swiss bank account, which would support his children and his 400,000 wives after he was executed and became a part of the Holy Trinity. The court ruled in November that Ford was competent to fire attorney LaJuana Davis and drop his appeals. Governor Don Siegelman rejected a clemency request filed by Davis, who cited Ford's history of mental problems.

Call for a Moratorium

The fundamental lack of due process for the mentally ill effectively results in the punishment of vulnerable persons for

their disabilities and for the failures of the courts to understand and protect them. Mentally ill persons who commit
crimes as a result of their brain disorders require treatment,
not punishment. The ACLU [American Civil Liberties Union]
calls for an immediate moratorium on the executions of mentally ill prisoners. Our laws, criminal justice practices, and a
sense of compassion should stand for the principle of justice
embodied in the Constitution's Eighth Amendment and in the
international human rights standards of the United Nations.

8

The Plea of Not Guilty by Reason of Insanity Should Remain Valid

Mental Health America

Mental Health America is a national nonprofit organization dedicated to promoting mental health and wellness, particularly for those living with mental illness.

The plea of not guilty by reason of insanity should remain an available legal option. "Guilty but insane" laws, which preclude the use of the insanity defense, are inappropriate and unfair because they force a criminal conviction and do not grant the accused any enforceable right to treatment. Individuals must be provided appropriate, recovery-based treatment rather than dealt with as if they have been found guilty.

Mental Health America is on record as supporting the maximum diversion from the criminal justice system of all persons accused of crimes for whom voluntary mental health treatment is a reasonable alternative to the use of criminal sanctions, at the earliest possible phase of the criminal process, preferably before booking or arraignment.

Further, Mental Health America has expressed skepticism concerning mental health court initiatives as they risk further criminalizing persons with mental illness. Mental Health America does not support mental health courts unless a particular court provides a meaningful alternative to criminal sanctions and meets the guidelines established in its position statement.

"Position Statement 57: In Support of the Insanity Defense," Mental Health America, March 7, 2004. Reproduced by permission.

Historically, Mental Health America has been a leader in supporting the insanity defense. In July 1982, when public interest was at its height following the acquittal of John Hinckley of the attempted assassination of President Reagan, on grounds of not guilty by reason of insanity, Mental Health America convened a panel of experts to examine the insanity defense. The panel was known as the National Commission on the Insanity Defense. The commission held public hearings, took testimony from more than twenty witnesses and, in March 1983, submitted its report and recommendations, entitled "Myths and Realities: A Report of the National Commission on the Insanity Defense." . . .

Mental illness is real, serious and treatable. Failure to recognize this results in unnecessary criminalization of persons with mental illness.

Mental Capacity Needed for Criminal Responsibility

Society has long recognized the need for judges and juries to discern which defendants are "criminally responsible" for their acts and which are not. The insanity defense refers to a defendant's plea that he or she is not guilty of a crime because he or she lacked the mental capacity to appreciate that what she or he did was wrong.

There have been many well-publicized court cases involving the insanity defense. Recent cases include the Andrea Yates case in Texas and the Russell Weston case in Washington, DC. These cases involve individuals who had been diagnosed with a mental illness and who committed crimes resulting in tragedies. When such cases arise, there is usually a discussion about the use of the insanity defense, its usefulness to society, and whether or not an individual is "faking" a mental illness to avoid a prison sentence. The public perception of the insanity defense is that it is overused and exploited.

The not guilty by reason of insanity test articulated by Section 4.01 is the most respected test for the insanity defense, and is endorsed by other national mental health advocacy organizations.

The reality is that the insanity defense is rarely used. The defense is, inevitably, less successful when community feeling is high and, given the certainty of involuntary treatment, it is rarely used in minor crimes. The implication that the insanity defense is used by "fakers" is disputed by the fact that in 80 percent of the cases where a defendant is acquitted on a "not guilty by reason of insanity" plea, the prosecution and defense have agreed on the appropriateness of the plea before the trial.

Mental illness is real, serious and treatable. Failure to recognize this results in unnecessary criminalization of persons with mental illness. Recognition of a broad form of the insanity defense is essential for the judicial system to address these issues.

The Model Penal Code

Mental Health America endorses the standards articulated in the American Law Institute's Model Penal Code, which represent the consensus of American legal scholars on the appropriate scope of the defenses of not guilty by reason of insanity and of not guilty on an element of the offense because of diminished capacity, and as a basis for clemency in capital cases if the accused's capacity was impaired due to mental illness at the time of the crime. . . . This position affirms that people suffering from a mental health crisis frequently have moral, rational, emotional and volitional impairments, all of which could provide a complete defense to a criminal charge, or, after conviction, a compelling factor precluding the death penalty. Mental health advocates and mental health associations should form coalitions to enact the Model Penal Code insanity and diminished capacity rules wherever they do not yet exist and to amend existing standards to better fit the Model Penal Code language wherever possible. . . .

Section 4.01

The not guilty by reason of insanity test articulated by Section 4.01 is the most respected test for the insanity defense, and is endorsed by other national mental health advocacy organizations. It has been expressly adopted in twenty-one states. While leaving room for emotional and moral "incapacity," it focuses on the rational and volitional tests, based on the principles that criminal conviction is not appropriate for an irrational or uncontrollable act. Most people would agree that such a person is beyond the reach of the restraining influence of the law. Thus, criminal conviction would be both futile and unjust.

The insanity defense goes back to [the case of Daniel] M'Naughten. . . . M'Naughten attempted to kill the Prime Minister of England but mistakenly killed the Prime Minister's secretary. His motivation for this attempted assassination was his belief that the Prime Minister was involved in a conspiracy to kill him. Due to his incapacity to appreciate the difference between right and wrong, M'Naughten was acquitted.

Thus, from the origins of the insanity defense, considerations of morality were combined with the factual question of whether or not the accused rationally appreciated the consequences of his or her act. And though the language of M'Naughten's case discouraged juries from focusing on non-cognitive impairments, on the boundary between rational appreciation and moral appreciation, an understanding was reached that the impaired emotional system of a person with serious mental illness going through a life crisis may not permit the person to appreciate the consequences of his or her act. Mental illness now is understood to entail moral, rational and emotional impairments, all of which bear on guilt or innocence if they impair the person's "substantial capacity" to "appreciate" the "wrongfulness" (the Model Penal Code's Reporter's preferred term) or "criminality" of the person's act. Thus, the insights of psychiatry concerning personal responsibility found their way into the courtroom. But all of these formulations failed to address the final element: the ability for the individual to have volitional control over his or her conduct. This element was added in later case law and legislation.

The American Law Institute's insanity defense rule, Section 4.01 of the Model Penal Code, is a consensus standard, based on the post-M'Naughten evolution of the case law. It uses the more global concept of "substantial capacity," which includes rational, moral and emotional capacity, and uses the noncognitive verb "to appreciate" rather than "to know" (giving deference to moral and emotional as well as rational insights), all of which are to be determined relative to the diagnosis of a "mental disease or defect" (left wisely undefined, "to accommodate developing medical understanding"). Thus, the Model Penal Code accommodates evolving diagnostic and treatment insights. Further, the Model Penal Code states that the capacity must relate either to the accused's ability to appreciate the criminality/wrongfulness of his or her conduct or to conform his or her conduct to the requirements of law, the volitional test. It should also be noted that the volitional test is completely separated from the "appreciation of criminality/wrongfulness" test, and a person may fully appreciate the criminality/wrongfulness of his or her act but be unable to control himself or herself under this formulation. This seems profoundly right.

Attacks on the Insanity Defense

The insanity defense has come under attack from several quarters, including the development of "guilty but insane" laws which deny the accused the right to claim insanity as a defense to the crime and permit only that the accused confess to the crime and seek to explain his or her conduct, requesting clemency through that process. This is the common traffic court plea of "guilty with an explanation." Yet people with mental illness who are convicted and treated pursuant to "guilty but insane" laws are not treated better, or granted any enforceable right to treatment. Defendants are inappropriately saddled with a criminal conviction, even if they would have been not guilty by reason of insanity under the consensus test of the Model Penal Code. For those who argue that the *mens rea* ["guilty mind"] defense survives, it should be understood that in crimes of negligence, there is no such defense. Thus, with guilty but insane, a conviction of some sort is assured, independent of the person's real responsibility/capacity. This seems profoundly unfair. Therefore, Mental Health America vigorously opposes "guilty but insane" laws.

The other attack has been of a more populist nature: seeking repeal of the insanity defense. In response to sensational cases, the public has become concerned about the notion that a person who committed a heinous crime may be adjudicated "not guilty." This is not surprising when studies are made that in popular belief, "the insane, through the insanity defense, escape punishment," that "an insanity defense is easily engineered," and that "the insanity defense places an unfair burden on the prosecution." According to the Commentary, the insanity defense is in fact very rarely invoked, and then only for very serious crimes—especially capital crimes. In fact, successful invocation of the insanity defense entails an indeterminate commitment to a mental health treatment facility, often with a standard much tougher than the civil commitment standard for release. And the defense is certainly not easy to make in practice.

The scholarly response to popular dissatisfaction with the insanity defense, ably fought by Goldstein and his intellectual progeny, has been to urge that the *mens rea* or "guilty mind" defense be used instead of the insanity defense, thus combining Sections 4.01 and 4.02 of the Model Penal Code. The great flaw in this idea is that crimes of negligence have no *mens rea* element. And M'Naughten himself would have been guilty under the *mens rea* test, since he clearly intended to kill, whether or not he was able to understand the wrongfulness of his conduct.

Mental Health America takes the position as a matter of policy that persons accused of crimes should be permitted to plead the insanity defense provided by Section 4.01 of the Model Penal Code as well as the defense of diminished capacity provided by Section 4.02 of the Model Penal Code. . . .

Impairment of capacity due to mental illness should weigh against imposition of the death penalty.

Section 4.02

The diminished capacity standard of Section 4.02(1) of the Model Penal Code has been criticized because it allows any evidence that the defendant may wish to present on the question of *mens rea*, notwithstanding the severity of the mental illness at issue. That having been said, the threshold of seriousness is probably a subject appropriately left to the discretion of the judge and jury, since even a transient illness or a limited impairment might have a significant impact on the individual's ability to appreciate the seriousness of a particular crime. And absent a countervailing value, it is appropriate to allow an accused to present all relevant evidence to a judge and jury, in the interest of justice.

Thus, the diminished capacity rule of Section 4.02(1) of the Model Penal Code also deserves support, although the issue of the seriousness of the mental illness which should be required in order to allow use of the defense will remain controversial. The concept of "serious mental illness" and prior formulations like "persistent" or "severe" have not expressed a clear scientific consensus on the issue of severity, and mental health professionals have not been able to make reliable distinctions between the different levels of impaired capacity experienced by persons with mental illness. The best course, therefore, seems to be to allow presentation of evidence about mental illness "whenever it is relevant to prove that the defendant did or did not have a state of mind that is an element of the offense," as required by Rule 4.02(1).

This is the *mens rea* defense, and it seems essential that it be preserved at every stage of the proceedings, as the modern critique of the insanity defense would do as well. But it should be noted that disproof of "guilty mind" is quite distinct from the moral, rational, emotional and volitional tests which are at the base of the insanity defense. As stated above, M'Naughten himself would have been guilty under the *mens rea* test. Thus, *mens rea* must be considered an independent legal principle to be applied in the admission of evidence dealing with mental illness, separate and distinct from the insanity defense. This is what Section 4.02(1) does.

For an organization on record in support of a death penalty moratorium, endorsement of Section 4.02(2) is self-evident. It is axiomatic that the Mental Health America supports admission of evidence concerning diminished capacity as an element in sentencing and that impairment of capacity due to mental illness should weigh against imposition of the death penalty.

Treatment

While beyond the scope of this policy, it is essential that successful invocation of the insanity defense be followed up with appropriate treatment as well as compassionate care during confinement and protection of human and civil rights. A person found not guilty should not be imprisoned, as a guilty person would be. It is also essential that recovery through treatment lead to release back to the community, although it is realistic to anticipate long delays in notorious cases. The treatment and release process should be removed from the criminal justice system and be placed in the clinical treatment process, and a comprehensive review of the person's mental health and recovery should be the basis for a finding of dangerousness or release. Psychiatric review boards are a promising model for such decisions.

9

Insanity Should Be a Medical, Not a Legal, Determination

Dirk Olin

Dirk Olin is director of the Institute for Judicial Studies and editor of JudicialReports.com.

The Washington, D.C.-area sniper, John Lee Malvo, a teenager, was convicted of murder despite pleading not guilty by reason of insanity. The insanity plea is a poor attempt to balance the public's need for accountability with a defendant's need for treatment. Decisions of guilt and mental health should be made separately. Juries are equipped to determine guilt, and doctors are qualified to make mental health determinations.

The jury in the trial of accused D.C.-area sniper John A. Muhammad has returned multiple guilty verdicts. [Next to be tried was] his alleged accomplice, teenager Lee Malvo. . . . The prosecution of the first case is essentially the defense in the second: that Malvo was merely following the demented orders of his father figure, Muhammad. To get that defense before the jury, Malvo [pleaded] not guilty by reason of insanity. [The jury rejected his insanity defense. He was convicted of murder and sentenced to life in prison.]

The very notion of a teenager crouched in the trunk of a car assassinating people willy-nilly does seem crazed on its face. But Malvo's courtroom tack has provoked the predictable outrage engendered by every attempt at the insanity plea. . . .

Dirk Olin, "Nuts to Whom? The Insanity Defense Is Crazy," *Slate.com*, November 18, 2003. Distributed by United Feature Syndicate, Inc. Reproduced by permission.

The Insanity Defense
Is Largely Misunderstood

Invocations of the insanity defense often pique the public because of a widespread misperception that the plea offers an opportunity to get away with murder. Such fears are almost completely groundless. Yet they've already led to the intellectually dishonest construct of "guilty but insane" pleas passed by legislatures in a number of states. These hybrid pleas promote a beguiling oversimplification of how society should apportion blame. Bright lines are often unavoidable in the law, but the precision of modern psychiatry demands that we stop asking juries to make medical determinations of insanity once and for all.

Malvo's plea is closer to that of Patty Hearst, the heiress kidnapped in the 1970s who took up bank robbery with her captors, than that of Jeffrey Dahmer, the cannibalistic mass murderer, or that of Andrea Yates, the postpartum depressive who drowned her five kids. Like Hearst, Malvo claims he was brainwashed, in his case by the older Muhammad. Juries typically put more stock in the concept of brainwashing than do members of the psychiatric field. Still, the jurors might prove tough to persuade in this case, if only because polls have shown that verdicts are more conditioned by jurors' visceral fear of the defendant than by their understanding of insanity's legal contours. And there's no question that Malvo's said some chilling stuff when interrogated about his part in the killing spree. So, Malvo now faces a two-part challenge: First, prove he was programmed into this serial monstrosity; second, evoke the jury's pity, or at least neutralize its terror of him.

The woolly-headed denunciations of the insanity defense are actually far more common than their invocation by criminal defendants. A reputable study funded by the National Institute of Mental Health in the early 1990s found this defense used in less than 1 percent of a representative sampling, with only one-quarter of those pleas argued successfully. (Hearst,

Dahmer, Yates, and even the Unabomber all failed with their insanity pleas, for example.) And even when such pleas do work, they almost never amount to a "get out of jail free" card. Studies show that an insanity pleader's average stay in a mental institution exceeds the average sentence served by those criminally convicted.

The "guilty but mentally ill" plea represents an ill-advised lurch toward a standard that feels both righteous and firm.

Origins of the Insanity Defense

Prior to the 19th century, guilt was more frequently judged according to causation than intent. If your cart ran over my foot, it didn't matter whether you meant to do it or not. You were adjudged blameworthy. As an appreciation of criminal motivation took hold, however, a door was opened to a greater variety of defenses. In 1843, the modern insanity defense was born after a Scottish psycho named Daniel M'Naughton tried to shoot British Prime Minister Sir Robert Peel, killing his secretary instead. A jury was persuaded by the testimony of various psychiatrists who said M'Naughton was delusional. The next year, a panel of judges created the standard that's been largely used in America ever since—that a defendant is not guilty if he or she didn't know what they were doing or didn't know it was wrong. (Competence to stand trial is weighed separately, because the defendant's mental state may have changed one way or the other since commission of the offense.)

Seems fair. But after John Hinckley was acquitted by reason of insanity in 1982—because he had shot President Reagan in an effort to impress actress Jodie Foster . . . various lawmakers started twitching. Reactionaries essentially equated insanity pleas with Twinkie defenses, and they wanted their

constituents to know they weren't going to stand for any mol-
lycoddling of criminals. So, many states passed statutes that
created pleas of "guilty but mentally ill." Under such systems
the deranged, if deemed guilty, are incarcerated in prisons
with "sane" inmates (though they may be accorded special
pharmaceutical arrangements). Failing to differentiate these
populations is like treating all illnesses with a blanket quaran-
tine. Whether any cures are possible is still an open question,
of course, but one we're much less likely to answer via unvar-
iegated warehousing.

It was society's previous failure to think through this issue
that made the system susceptible to such ineffectual changes.
The "guilty but mentally ill" plea represents an ill-advised
lurch toward a standard that feels both righteous and firm.
But out of an understandable desire to heighten accountability
came a logical absurdity: You're guilty—but you're not. You
are sick and thus not wholly accountable, yet you are treated
exactly the same as the guilty. The mutual contradiction inherent in such a construct takes the "oxy" out of oxymoronic.

---

*The system should separate medical diagnoses from legal
judgments.*

Do the semantics of all this really matter for purposes of
our criminal justice system? If the goal is to protect us against
violent perps, does it make a difference whether we call them
nuts or no-good? It might. A recent study by Human Rights
Watch concluded that as many as one in five of the 2.1 million Americans in jail and prison are seriously mentally ill.
That's roughly five times the number of people in mental hospitals. The far-ranging lack of appropriate therapy can hardly
be reducing recidivism, and it certainly carries no deterrence
for mentally ill criminals. It also fails to meet the retributive
goal of reserving punishment for the guilty.

A Proposed Solution

One modest solution? The system should separate medical diagnoses from legal judgments. We should employ disinterested experts—appointed by the court, rather than hired by otherwise appropriately adversarial players—to address such questions empirically, as opposed to strategically. Insanity has historically been a legal, not medical, term. Junk it. If a defendant claims mental illness, better to let a panel of psychiatric professionals parse the severity of any condition than leave it to the vicissitudes of a jury. (Defendants need not waive right to trial: If they are determined to be sane, the fact-finding would go forward; if not, they could reach a plea deal based on the medical panel's finding.)

Juries are impaneled to try facts. Judges are responsible for interpreting the law. A jury shouldn't diagnose Lee Malvo's maladies (or lack thereof), any more than it should rule on evidentiary admissibility or perform tonsillectomies. If we lock up violent offenders without understanding why they did what they did, we vitiate the meaning of retribution, which society demands. We also mitigate the possibility of rehabilitation, which basic humanism requires. We can, of course, choose to continue ignoring this problem, locking up more and more insane defendants while treating them less and less.

But that way madness lies.

10

Television Dramas Lead to Discussion of Mental Health and Crime

Rachel Gans-Boriskin and Claire Wardle

Rachel Gans-Boriskin teaches at the University of Pennsylvania. Claire Wardle is a lecturer at the Cardiff University School of Journalism, Media, and Cultural Studies in Wales. Her research examines the ways in which social and political issues are represented in different media formats.

Law & Order, *and other shows with a "ripped from the headlines" format elaborate upon controversial social issues in ways that nonfiction media do not. These shows influence society's perception of such issues, including mental illness.*

The NBC network publicizes many of its primetime shows with the tagline 'ripped from the headlines' because it draws its themes and plotlines from news stories and current events. *Law & Order* was the original 'ripped from the headlines' show, but the trend of high-quality fictional programming that draws on real life events has been replicated across networks with shows such as *West Wing*, *The Practice*, *ER* and *Third Watch*. We argue these programs represent the emergence of a new and distinct format of fictional television drama that provides revealing insights about cultural responses to social and political issues, and offers a fertile area for research. . . .

Rachel Gans-Boriskin and Claire Wardle, "Mad or Bad? Negotiating the Boundaries of Mental Illness on *Law & Order*," *Journal of Criminal Justice and Popular Culture*, vol. 12, no. 1, 2005, pp. 26–46. © 2005 School of Criminal Justice, University at Albany. Reproduced by permission.

Mental Illness in the Media

Much of the research about the portrayal of mental illness in the media bemoans the fact that [according to Dr. Julio Arboleda Florez], "the general public most frequently makes contact with mental illness through the media and movies. Unfortunately the media often depicts patients as unpredictable, violent and dangerous." *Law & Order* episodes feature defendants who suffer from various forms of mental illness on a fairly frequent basis, but the primary focus in this paper is not examining how the mentally ill are portrayed, but rather the ways in which mental illness is used to discuss larger societal questions.

There has been a significant amount of research on images of the mentally ill in the mass media. This research has shown that the public receives the majority of its information about mental illness and the mentally ill from the mass media. Research into the depictions of the mentally ill in the media, both factual and fictitious, is substantial. Much of the research has involved content analyses of different media outlets that have examined whether mental illness is considered at all and, if so, how those who suffer are portrayed. These studies repeatedly demonstrate that mass media depictions of mental illness are overwhelmingly negative. While discussions about how mental illnesses are portrayed in the mass media are increasing, negative depictions of the mentally ill mean that ignorance about mental health issues persists. Similarly, there is still considerable concern about the continued problem of the stigma associated with these illnesses and those who suffer from them. In a comprehensive literature review of studies in mass media images of mental illness, [Dr. Otto F.] Wahl demonstrates that mental illness is the most commonly depicted disability. One in every ten disabilities shown involves a mental health or psychological topic. The most common depictions of the mentally ill are that they lack social identity, are single, unemployed, dangerous, and unpredictable. More recent studies into common misperceptions about mental illness show again that the overwhelming negative stereotype is that the mentally ill are dangerous and violent. . . .

The *Law & Order* Format Encourages Discussion

In [a] sample of seven episodes, we found that three themes emerged in discussions related to the subject of mental illness. The episodes we studied argued about specific concerns such as the effect of abuse in determining an individual's psyche, existential questions about the nature of good and evil, and institutional fears about the court's ability to handle the mentally ill.

> The ripped from the headlines format allows the writers to move beyond the rigidity of news reporting that demands the 'who, what, where, and when', while drawing on storylines that are familiar to viewers because they have seen them elsewhere.

The program writers have consistently stated that they want to make people think about the issues presented in the shows. It is thus interesting to look at the ways in which the writers have chosen to explore the issues of mental illness, personal responsibility, and crime and punishment. The [Not Guilty by Reason of Insanity] NGRI defense allows these wider discussions because it allows an individual, due to a mental defect, to avoid punishment because of a different level of culpability [responsibility]. It presents an ambiguous moment in the criminal justice system. The fact that this is a legal drama with half the program based in the courtroom allows the scriptwriters to explore the issues from either side, forcing the prosecution and defense to consider these issues from different perspectives with eloquent and thoughtful dialogue. We believe this dramatic format encourages dialogue among viewers in ways that may not be the case with the news.

This research raises three valuable issues. First it demonstrates the need for more sophisticated analyses of the portrayal of mental illness, beyond content analyses that quantify positive and negative images. Qualitative discourse analysis allows a more nuanced understanding of how specific topics are considered. Second, the research shows the freedom provided by fictional formats, particularly these ripped from the headlines dramas, to cover issues in ways that could spark conversation and discussions. Third, the questions raised by the show about the nature of mental illness and how it relates to issues of personal responsibility and criminal behavior, as well as the problems of scarcity of resources for mental health in the criminal justice system, are not commonly addressed in other public arenas in society.

The ripped from the headlines format allows the writers to move beyond the rigidity of news reporting that demands the 'who, what, where, and when', while drawing on storylines that are familiar to viewers because they have seen them elsewhere. As [James W.] Carey has explained, the demands of the four easy to answer 'w's' means that the most important, but often most different 'w' (the 'why'), frequently gets ignored. In the famous *Law & Order* format of two halves, the first half of the seven episodes mimicked the focus of news coverage with its emphasis on the investigation of fact, whereas the second half moved beyond the realms of typical journalism and asked questions about why an individual committed a crime and to what extent the society in which s/he lived was responsible for those actions. In addition, the show considered how society should deal with those people who fall outside the range of normal and whether the ultimate purpose of the criminal justice system is rehabilitation or retribution.

According to [Doris] Graber's study, 25% of newspaper stories and 20% of television stories are related to crime. Despite the dedication of the news media to crime related topics, wider questions are almost totally absent from mainstream reporting. If news does not address these questions, where should society turn? Partly because of a cultural climate that demands stricter and harsher punishment for criminals, the ethical and moral questions inherent in these cases are obscured and ignored. Politicians do not want to be seen as soft on crime, providing a disincentive to encourage debate about the flaws in the system. The absence of thoughtful discussion exacerbates the problem, encouraging criminal justice policy to be shaped by knee jerk reactions to highly publicized but usually anomalous crimes.

Fictional programs like *Law & Order* hold privileged positions as they are able to discuss the problems of the criminal justice system without fearing the political consequences. As a fictional character, Jack McCoy can consider controversial arguments in a way that politicians in the state or federal legislature are unable, making impassioned pleas without fearing that he will lose votes at the polls.

We are not arguing that the shows themselves are not influenced by societal pressure. Although raising critical questions, the show does not propose radical solutions. As our sample demonstrates, the majority of the discourse around the NGRI pleas falls into the category of 'the con,' suggesting that many of the mental disorders discussed are not worthy of serious consideration. Furthermore, most of the defendants in the episodes were convicted, thereby continuously maintaining the status quo.

Despite these qualifications, the episodes are encouraging viewers to engage in discussions that are rarely happening elsewhere and are involved in the negotiation of meaning over where the boundaries should fall in terms of what society will accept as mental illness. Inherent in these arguments is the recognition that the acceptance of mental illness is socially constructed. Mental illnesses that are now considered legitimate were ridiculed twenty years ago. As society changes with progress in the diagnosis and treatment of mental illness, the definitions of mental illness are evolving. At times there is a discrepancy between what is accepted by psychiatry and what society, at large, is willing to acknowledge. *Law & Order* probes those areas on the borders of legitimacy and uses them to ask pointed questions about the consequences of broadening definitions of mental illness.

It appears that *Law & Order* uses mental illness as a foil for discussing larger societal issues. By addressing social problems through the lens of mental illness, the programs allow people to gain critical distance from issues so that they might examine tendencies in their own behavior in a non-threatening way. In this way, the programs in our sample are only partly about mental illness. In many respects they are about locating deviance in 'the other' and exploring to what extent that deviance is shared.

Limitations of the Show's Format

We believe it is a positive development that *Law & Order* is addressing these issues, as so few other arenas in society are doing so. However, the limitations of the fictional format also need to be addressed. The stories are compelling from both a cultural and dramatic perspective, and it is ultimately the theatrical nature of the stories that results in the writers consistently returning to these plotlines.

A primary concern is that mental illness as a medical condition may be de-legitimized. One of the themes was the idea that mental illness is used in the justice system to avoid personal responsibility for committing crime. Indeed, the frequency of the Not Guilty by Reason of Insanity plea is grossly overrepresented in *Law & Order*. Whereas the NGRI plea was made in 7% of *Law & Order* episodes, the plea is actually offered between 0.9% and 1.5% of the time. Research carried out by Wahl demonstrated a perception that the public tends to overestimate the frequency and the success rate of the NGRI defense. Such a disproportionate representation may exaggerate in people's minds the frequency of the defense and may create the impression that criminals are not being punished due to the plea.

Research is clear that violent depictions of the mentally ill influence attitudes towards those who suffer from mental disorders.

In our sample, many of the cases resulted in a conviction for the defendant. The NGRI pleas failed for several reasons. In some cases, the characters bemoaned the rigidity of the law in not accommodating people who clearly are mentally ill, but do not reach the legal standard of insanity. In other cases, the mental illness is considered illegitimate or not rising to the level necessary to negate personal responsibility. The frequency of such depictions may perpetuate the notion that psychiatry and psychology are leading to phony diagnoses. This would undermine efforts to educate society about the prevalence of mental illness in the hope of lessening the stigma attached to these disorders.

Stigma is certainly attached when depictions of mental illness stress the violent nature of the mentally ill. Although *Law & Order* may raise important questions about mental health and its treatment system, it does so in the context of cases where the mentally ill individual has committed a murder. Furthermore, *Law & Order*'s depictions of the mentally ill must be understood in the context of a television environment that consistently portrays the mentally ill as dangerous. Research is clear that violent depictions of the mentally ill influence attitudes towards those who suffer from mental disorders. It may also contribute to a belief that crime is disproportionately committed by people with mental illnesses. Finally, research on perceptions of the NGRI defense illustrate that people remained concerned about their safety as a result of the use of the defense. A common belief is that the defense results in offenders being placed in mental hospitals rather than prisons, allowing them early release. Discussions on *Law & Order* about the flaws in the system, including overcrowding, incorrect diagnoses, and appropriate rehabilitation, only add to these concerns.

The nature of formula television compels the writers of *Law & Order* to frequently deliver a guilty verdict to the audience. The drama builds by following a crime through the criminal justice system and it would be dramatically unsettling if the prosecutors, some of the main characters, consistently lost. The title *Law & Order* also demonstrates the ideological direction in which the viewers should expect the show to lean. It would be a surprise if the episodes concluded with plotlines that provided anything else. Furthermore, as social control theory would predict, the neat endings to the programs allow viewers to leave the program without feeling threatened that mentally ill people are being released on to the streets or that criminals are getting away with murder by feigning mental illness. In this way, even though *Law & Order* asks difficult questions, it ultimately provides comforting answers.

The Need for Future Research

As the preceding discussion clearly illustrates, there is a considerable amount to be learned from examining the ways that fictional media discuss and depict mental illness and larger societal questions. The writers of television fiction are engaging in substantive discussions of issues and we believe that more studies are needed to explore the ways in which members of the public discuss the issues raised in these fictional programs. Ethnographic and focus group research that examines the specific ways in which people talk and negotiate meaning during and after viewing these shows, particularly as they relate to mental illness and crime and punishment is needed. Such research would be helpful in understanding the ways in which people use media to form their opinions and views of reality. As the implosion of format and genre distinctions becomes an acknowledged characteristic of contemporary television programming and these 'ripped from the headlines' shows remain popular, this particular format will hopefully receive more attention.

Organizations to Contact

The editors have compiled the following list of organizations concerned with the issues debated in this book. The descriptions are derived from materials provided by the organizations. All have publications or information available for interested readers. The list was compiled on the date of publication of the present volume; the information provided here may change. Be aware that many organizations take several weeks or longer to respond to inquiries, so allow as much time as possible.

The Carter Center
One Copenhill, Atlanta, GA   30307
(404) 420-5100
e-mail: carterweb@emory.edu
Web site: www.cartercenter.org/health/
mental_health/index.html

Founded by former first lady Rosalynn Carter, the mental health division of the Carter Center works to promote awareness, health care, and programs that support those suffering from mental illnesses and to reduce the stigma and discrimination against them. The Carter Center hosts two public-policy forums each year for those in the mental health field as well as public outreach programs. The Center also sponsors fellowships for journalists.

Citizens Commission on Human Rights
6616 Sunset Boulevard, Los Angeles, CA   90028
(323) 467-4242 • fax: (323) 467-3720
e-mail: humanrights@cchr.org
Web site: www.cchr.org

Created by the Church of Scientology, the Citizens Commission on Human Rights (CCHR) is a nonprofit organization dedicated to investigating and exposing psychiatric violations of human rights. It also ensures that criminal acts within the psychiatric industry are reported to the proper authorities and acted upon. CCHR's board of advisors includes doctors, scientists, psychologists, lawyers, legislators, educators, business professionals, celebrities, and civil and human rights representatives.

Criminal Justice/Mental Health Consensus Project
100 Wall Street, 20th Floor, New York, NY   10005
(212) 482-2320 • fax: (212) 482-2344
e-mail: cp_editors@consensusproject.org
Web site: www.consensusproject.org

The Criminal Justice/Mental Health Consensus Project, coordinated by the Council of State Governments Justice Center, is a national effort to help local, state, and federal policy makers and criminal justice and mental health professionals improve the response to people with mental illnesses who come into contact with the criminal justice system. The Consensus Project Report was released in June 2002. Since then, the Consensus Project has supported practical, flexible criminal justice/mental health strategies through on-site technical assistance, the dissemination of information about programs, research, policy developments, policy recommendations, and educational presentations.

International Justice Project
6 Allerton Court, Bishop Auckland, County Durham
   DL13 2FB
   England
+1 (0)1388-527-403 • fax: +1 (0)1388-528-647
e-mail: info@internationaljusticeproject.org
Web site: www.internationaljusticeproject.org

The International Justice Project (IJP) works to develop, coordinate, and increase use of international law and human rights standards as they pertain to capital punishment. The IJP advocates for the abolition of the death penalty in the United States and provides briefs, information, and education in support of its mission.

Mental Health America
2000 N. Beauregard Street, 6th Floor, Alexandria, VA   22311
(703) 684-7722 • fax: (703) 684-5968
Web site: www.mentalhealthamerica.net

Mental Health America (MHA), formerly known as the National Mental Health Association, is a nonprofit organization dedicated to helping all people live mentally healthier lives. With more than 320 affiliates nationwide, MHA promotes the mental well-being of the nation, daily and in times of crisis. MHA promotes education, research, and policy to raise awareness and assist the needs of those suffering from mental illness.

National Alliance on Mental Illness
Colonial Place Three, Arlington, VA   22201-3042
(703) 524-7600 • fax: (703) 524-9094
Web site: www.nami.org

The National Alliance on Mental Illness (NAMI) is a grassroots organization for people with mental illness and their families. Founded in 1979, NAMI has affiliates in every state and in more than 1,100 local communities across the country. NAMI is dedicated to the eradication of mental illnesses and to the improvement of the quality of life for persons of all ages who are affected by mental illnesses via support, education, and advocacy.

National Institute of Mental Health
National Institute of Mental Health (NIMH)
Bethesda, MD   20892-9663
(866) 615-6464 • fax: (301) 443-4279
e-mail: nimhinfo@nih.gov
Web site: www.nimh.nih.gov

The National Institute of Mental Health (NIMH) is a governmental, scientific organization that supports research about the understanding, treatment, and prevention of mental disorders and the promotion of mental health. Its mission is to transform the understanding and treatment of mental illnesses through research, paving the way for prevention, recovery, and cure.

**Substance Abuse and Mental Health
Services Administration**
1 Choke Cherry Road, Rockville, MD   20857
(877) 726-4727
Web site: www.samhsa.gov

The Substance Abuse and Mental Health Services Administration (SAMHSA) works to improve the quality and availability of substance abuse prevention, alcohol and drug addiction treatment, and mental health services for everyone. To realize this mission, SAMHSA gears its programs, policies, and grants toward building resilience and facilitating recovery for people with or at risk for mental or substance use disorders.

Treatment Advocacy Center
200 N. Glebe Road, Suite 730, Arlington, VA   22203
(703) 294-6001 • fax: (703) 294-6010
e-mail: info@treatmentadvocacycenter.org
Web site: www.treatmentadvocacycenter.org

The Treatment Advocacy Center (TAC) is a national nonprofit organization that aims to eliminate barriers to timely and effective treatment for people with severe psychiatric illnesses who are not receiving appropriate medical care. TAC involves itself in court cases, legislative debate, education, and public opinion. TAC frequently publishes reports on its findings, and its founder, E. Fuller Torrey, recently wrote the book *The Insanity Offense.*

Bibliography

Books

Heather Ahn-Redding	*The Insanity Defense the World Over.* Lanham, MD: Lexington Books, 2008.
Phillip Bean	*Madness and Crime.* Uffculme, UK: Willan, 2008.
Charlie Bronson	*Insanity: My Mad Life.* London: John Blake, 2004.
Russell Eisenman	*Creativity, Mental Illness, and Crime.* Dubuque, IA: Kendall Hunt, 2008.
Patricia E. Erickson and Steven K. Erickson	*Crime, Punishment, and Mental Illness.* Piscataway, NJ: Rutgers University Press, 2008.
Charles Patrick Ewing	*Insanity: Murder, Madness, and the Law.* New York: Oxford University Press, 2008.
Ellsworth L. Fersch	*Thinking About the Insanity Defense: Answers to Frequently Asked Questions with Case Examples.* iUniverse, 2005.
Mary Beth Pfeiffer	*Crazy in America: The Hidden Tragedy of Our Criminalized Mentally Ill.* New York: Basic Books, 2007.

| Christina Hoff Sommers | *One Nation Under Therapy: How the Helping Culture Is Eroding Self-Reliance.* New York: St. Martin's Griffin, 2006. |

| E. Fuller Torrey | *The Insanity Offense: How America's Failure to Treat the Seriously Mentally Ill Endangers Its Citizens.* New York: Norton, 2008. |

| Corey J. Vitello and Eric W. Hickey | *The Myth of a Psychiatric Crime Wave: Public Perception, Juror Research, and Mental Illness.* Durham, NC: Carolina Academic Press, 2006. |

| Rebecca Woolis | *When Someone You Love Has a Mental Illness.* New York: Penguin, 2003. |

Periodicals

| Amnesty International USA | "Another Texas Injustice: The Case of Kelsey Patterson, Mentally Ill Man Facing Execution," 2004. |

| The Associated Press | "Arizona Case Puts Insanity Defense Under Fire," *MSNBC*, April 19, 2006. |

| Emily Bazelon | "Crazy Law: The Supreme Court Beats Up on the Insanity Defense," *Slate*, July 6, 2006. |

| Ralph Blumenthal | "A Growing Plea for Mercy for the Mentally Ill on Death Row," *New York Times*, November 23, 2006. |

Diane Carman   "Pull Curtain on Political Tragedy: Jailing the Mentally Ill," *Denver Post*, December 6, 2006.

Ariane DeVouge   "Executing Mentally Ill Goes to Highest Court," *ABC News*, April 18, 2007.

Gary Fields   "On Death Row, Fate of Mentally Ill Is a Problem," *Pittsburgh Post-Gazette*, December 14, 2006.

Frontline   "From Daniel M'Naughten to John Hinckley: A Brief History of the Insanity Defense." www.pbs.org/ wgbh/pages/frontline/shows/crime/ trial/history.html.

John Gibeaut   "A Matter Over Mind," *ABA Journal*, April 2006.

Sarah Rosenfield, Julie Phillips, and Helene White   "Gender, Race, and the Self in Mental Health and Crime," *Social Problems*, vol. 53, no. 2, 2006.

Irwin Savodnik   "Psychiatry's Sick Compulsion: Turning Weaknesses into Diseases," *Los Angeles Times*, January 1, 2006.

South Florida Sun-Sentinel   "Dream of Dignity Collides with Reality," February 15, 2004.

Steve Twedt   "Lack of Options Keep Mentally Disturbed Youth Locked Up," *Pittsburgh Post-Gazette*, July 2001.

Sam Vaknin   "The Insanity of the Defense," *Global Politician*, May 1, 2005.

Index

A

Adams, Lorraine, 50

Akathisia (psychomotor restlessness), 37

Alabama, 64

American Bar Association, 62

American Civil Liberties Union (ACLU), 57–66

American Law Institute's Model Penal Code, 68–75

American Psychiatric Association, 37

Antidepressant drugs, 64

Antidepressant Fact Book (Breggin), 38

Antipsychotic drugs, 37–39

Anxiety disorders, 13

Arkansas, 62–63

B

Battered women's syndrome, 50

Bazelon Center for Mental Health Law, 42–43, 46–47

Beltway Sniper, 8

   See also Malvo, John Lee

Bipolar disorder, 11, 13, 40, 45, 57

Bobbit, Commonwealth v., 49–53

Bobbit, Lorena, 8, 49–53

Borderline personality disorder, 57

Breggin, Peter, 34–38

Bureau of Justice Statistics, 58–59

C

Care in the Community policies, 21

   See also Community mental health care programs

Carey, James W., 84

Center for Behavioral Health, Justice and Public Policy, 41

Cho, Seung-Hui, 34–39

Civil liberties/rights, 14, 74

   See also Due process; Human rights

Colburn, James Blake, 64

Columbine (Colorado) school shootings, 38

Commonwealth v. Bobbit, 49–53

Community mental health care programs, 44, 46–47

   See also Care in the Community policies

Consensus Project, 45–46

Copycat crimes, 33

Criminal Justice/Mental Health Consensus Project report (2002), 45–46

Culpability. *See* Individual responsibility

D

Dahmer, Jeffrey, 77–78

Davis, LaJuana, 65

Davis, Patricia, 50

Davoli, Joanmarie Ilaria, 50–53

Day, Kenneth, 20–21

Death penalty, 8, 59–66, 73–74